MW01126286

HUMMINGBIRDS COLORING BOOK!

DISCOVER THIS COLLECTION OF COLORING PAGES FOR KIDS

Bold Illustrations
COLORING BOOKS

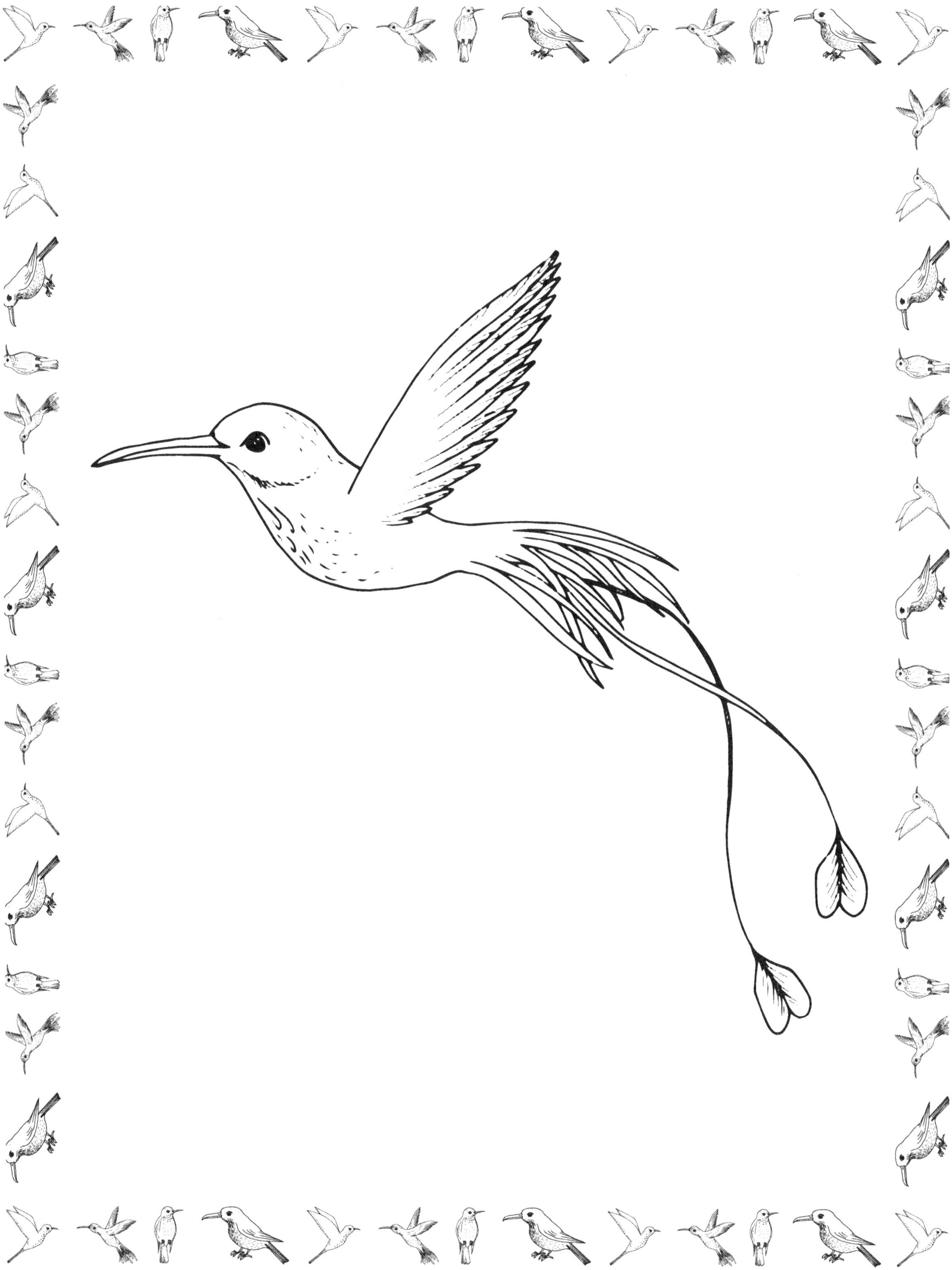

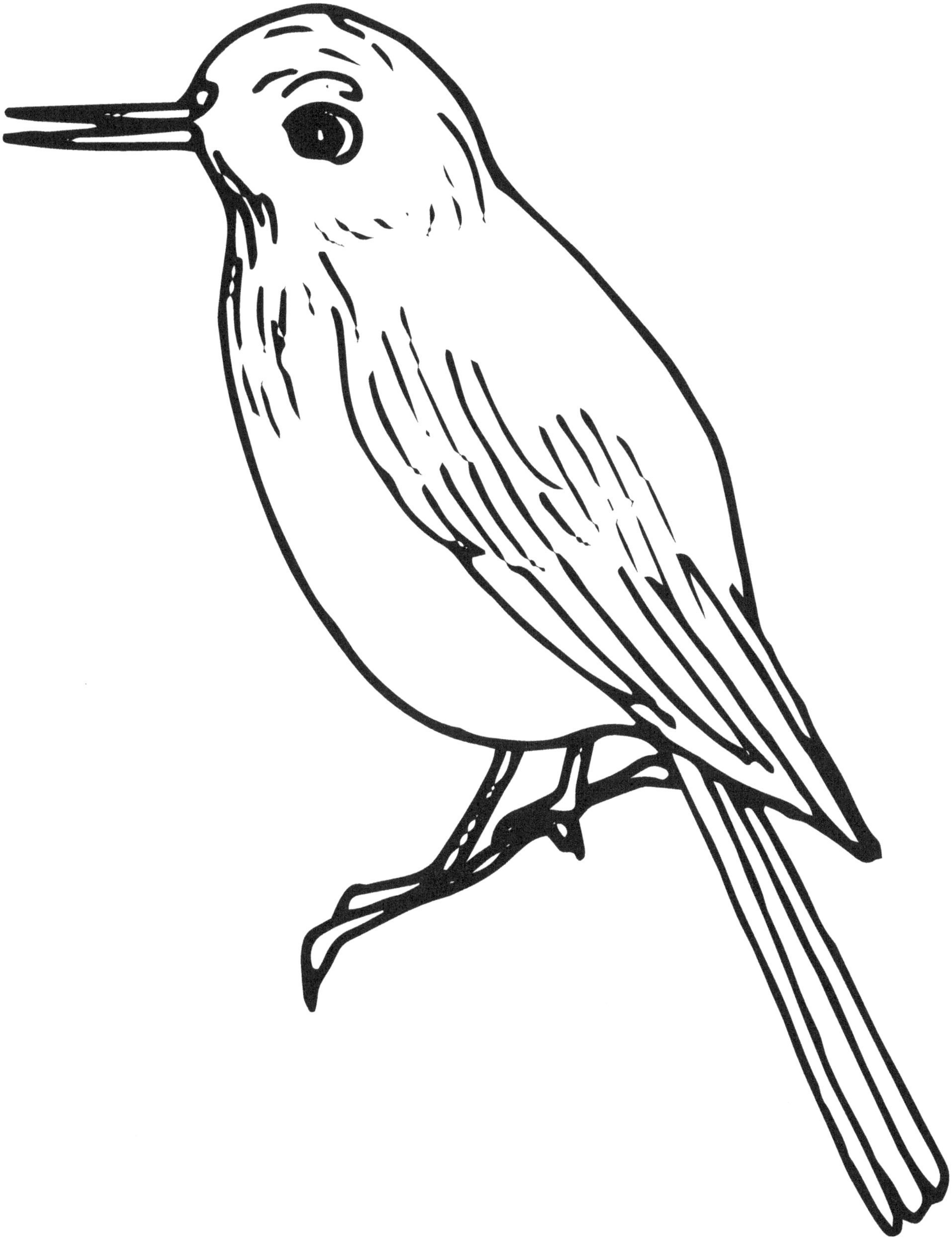

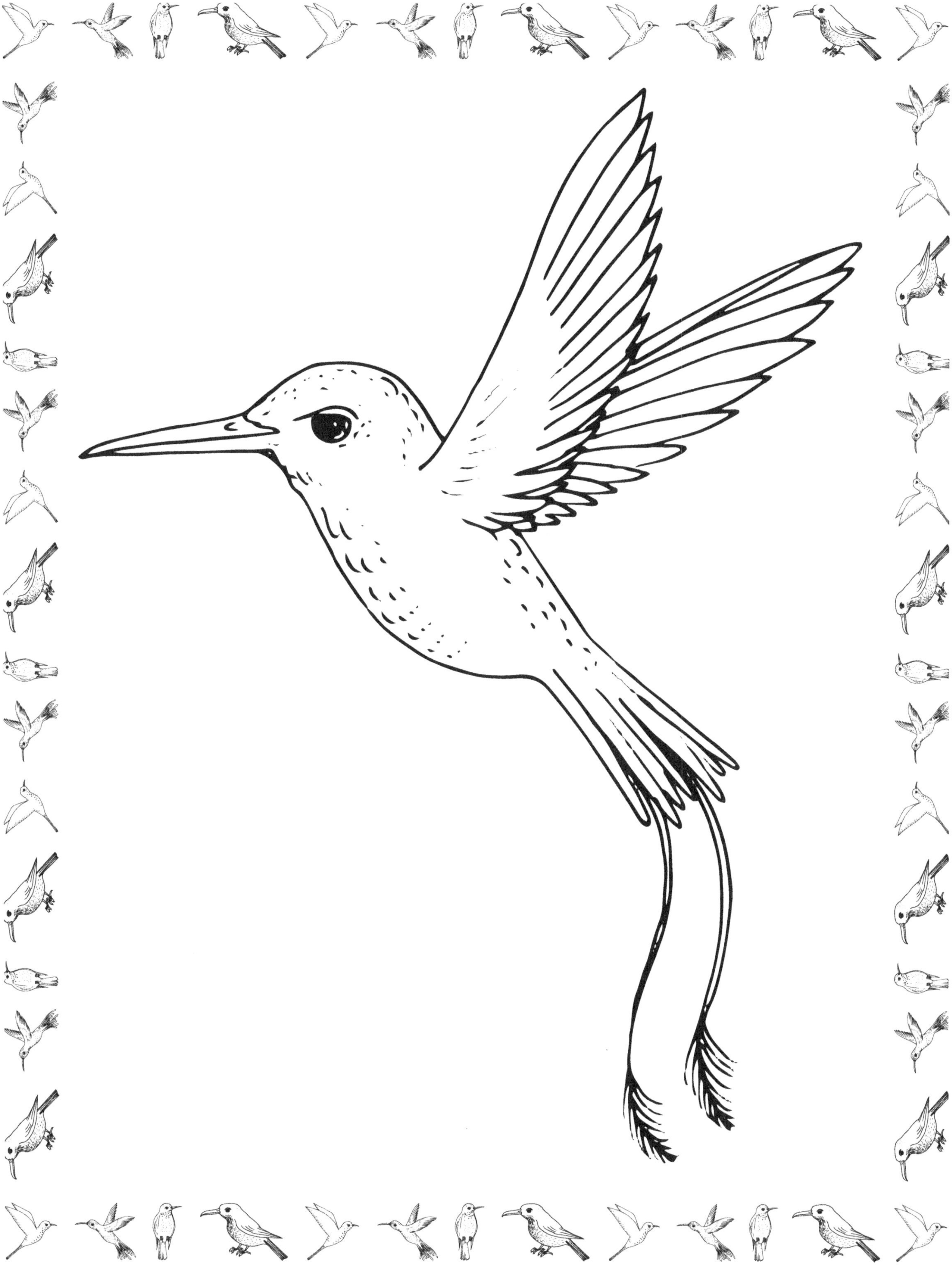

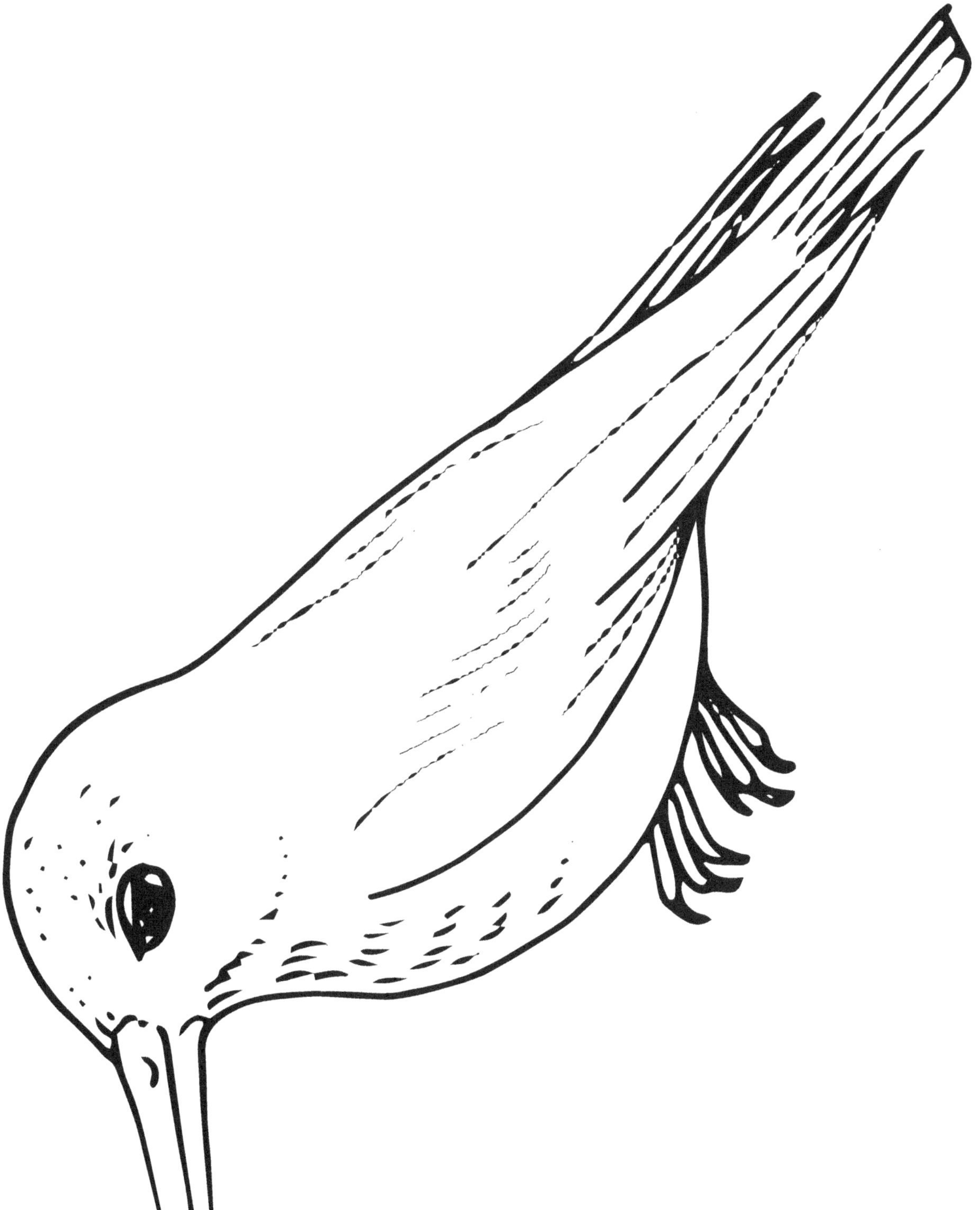

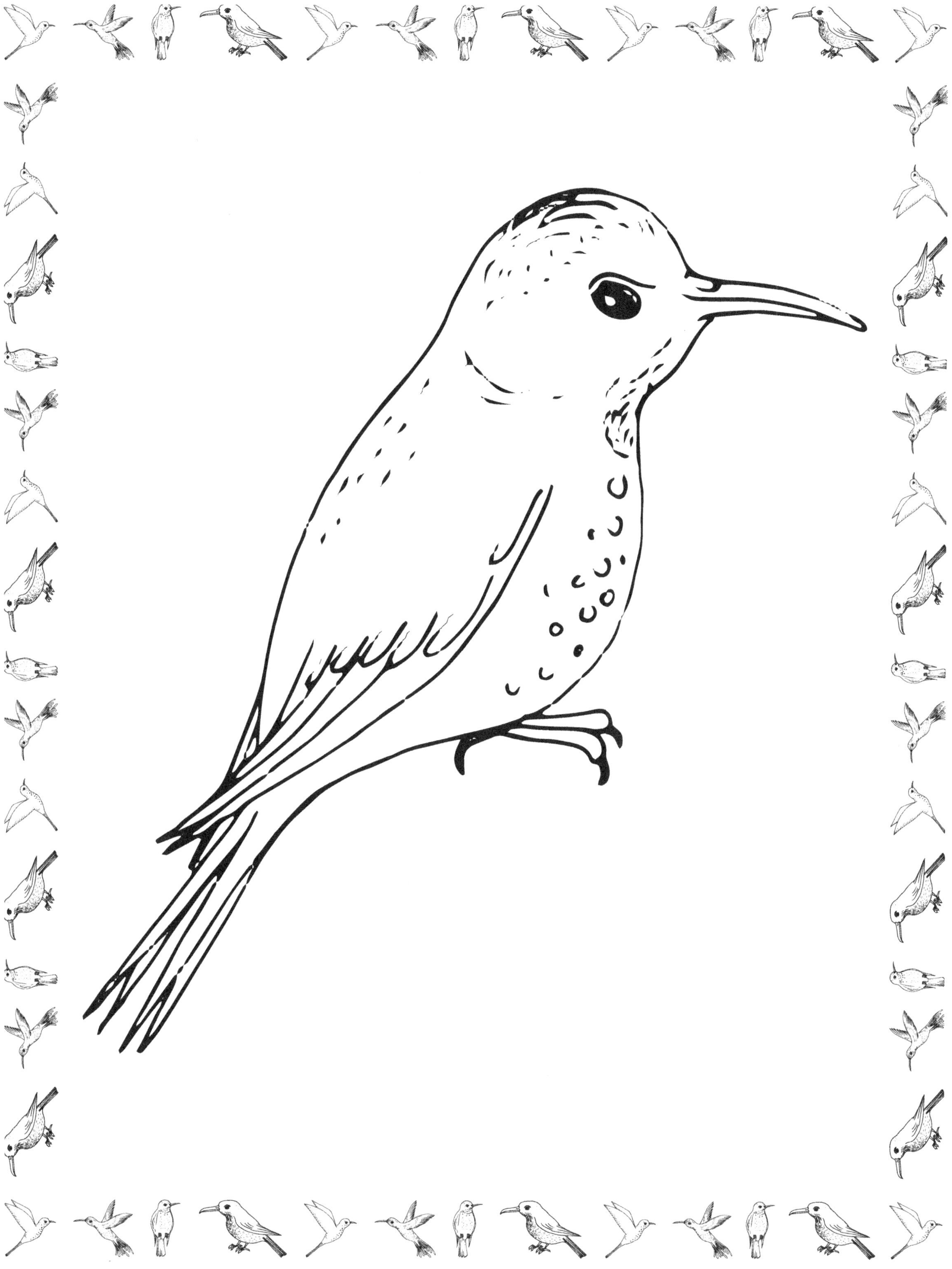

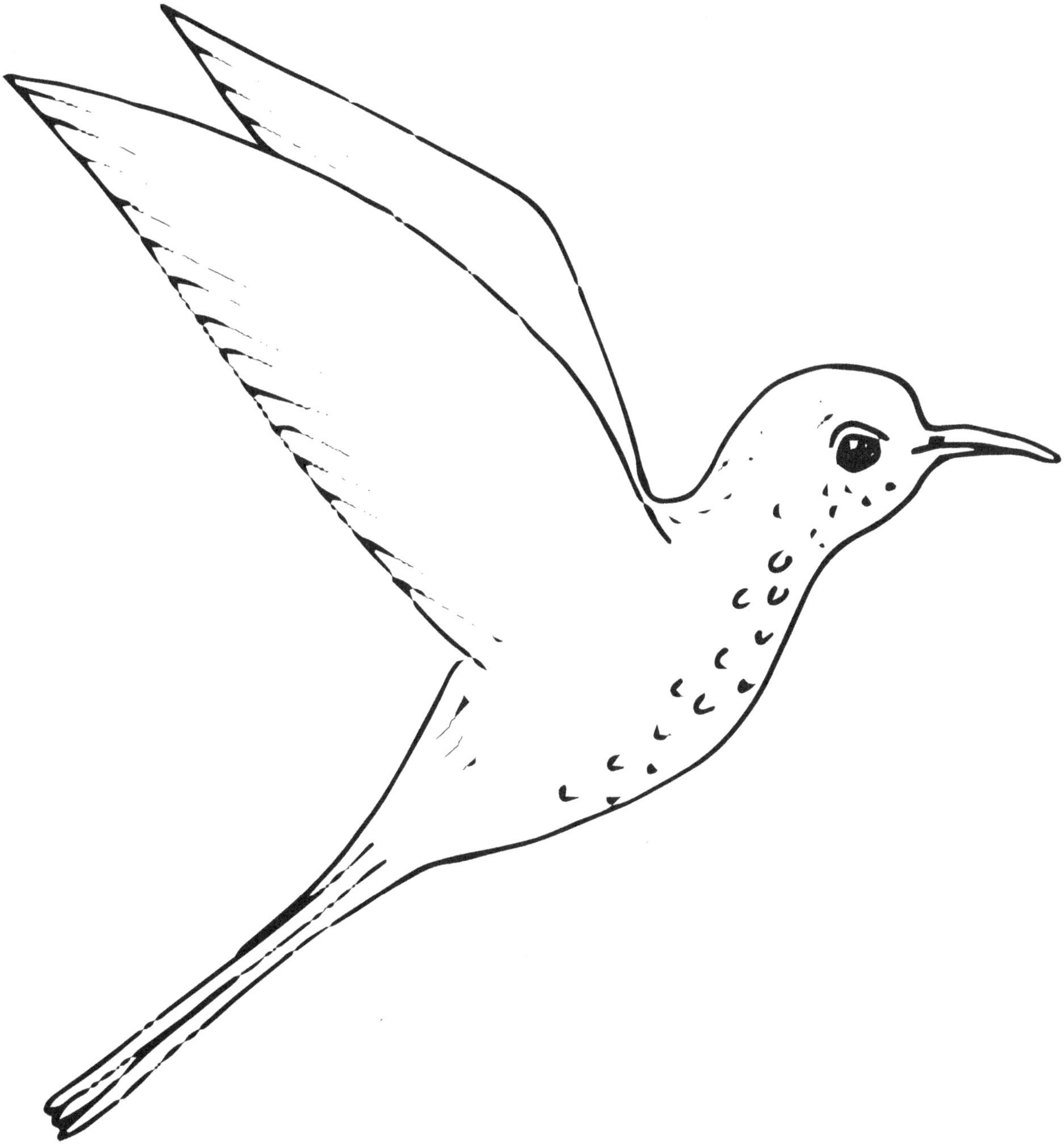

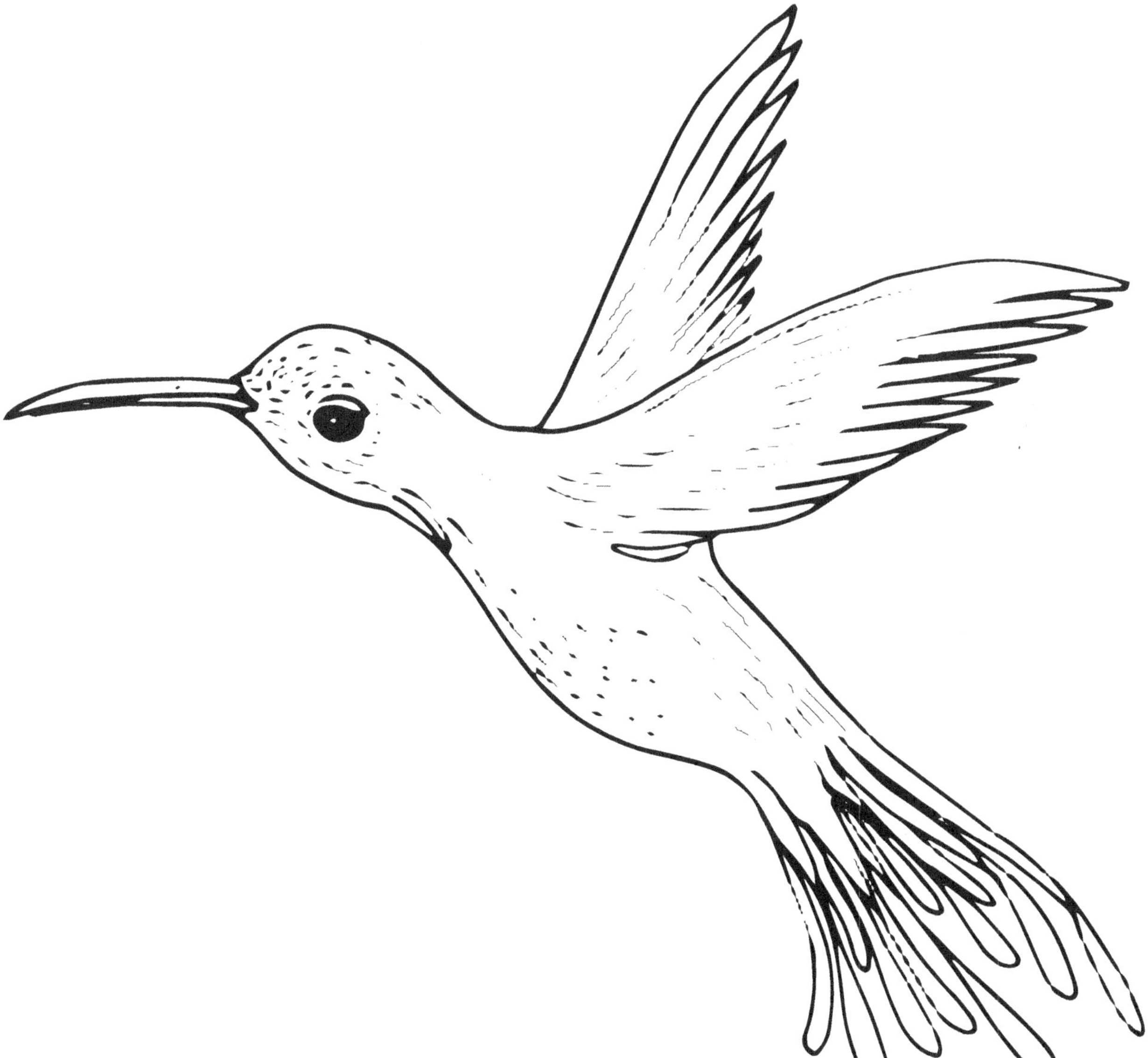

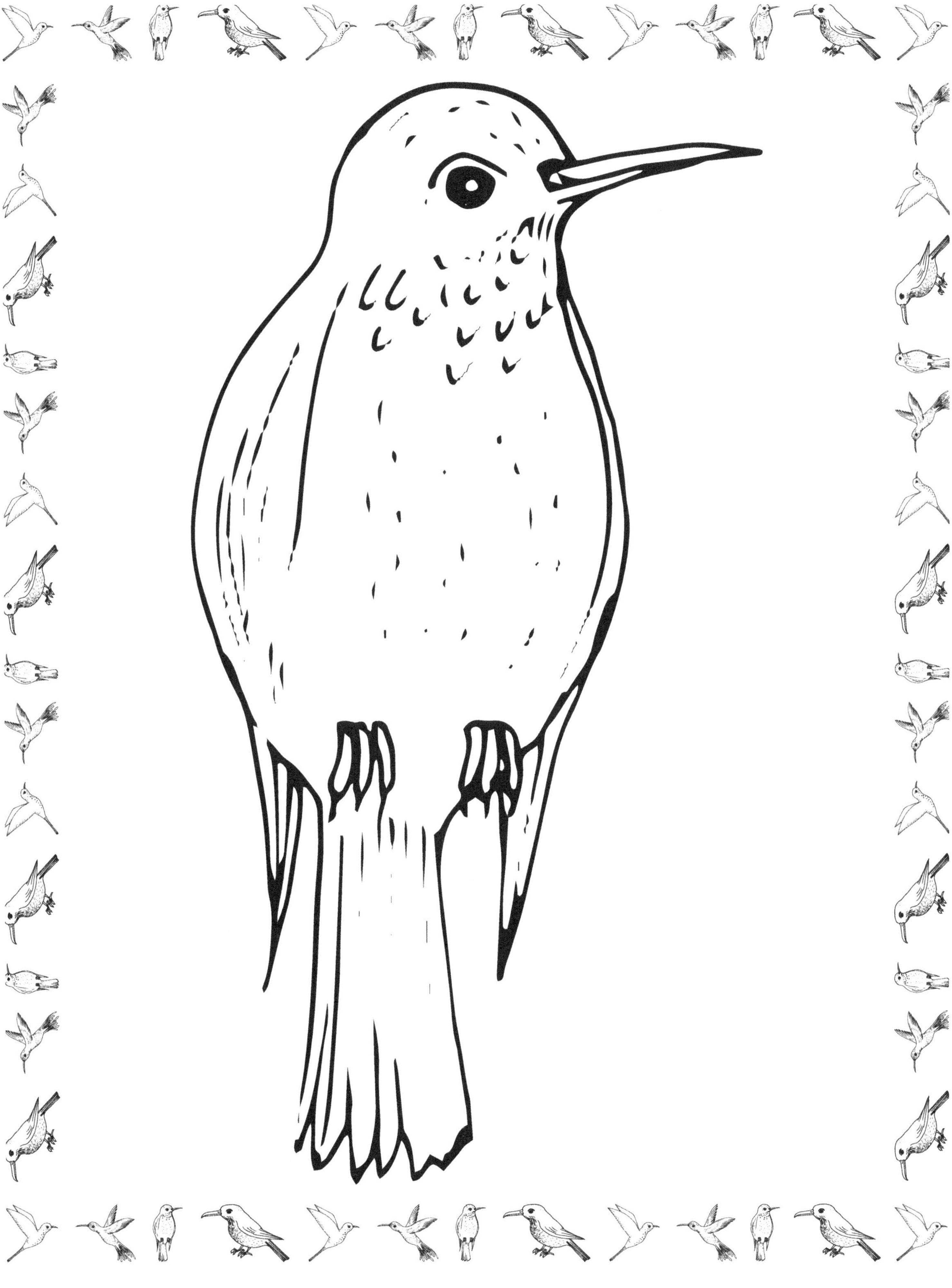

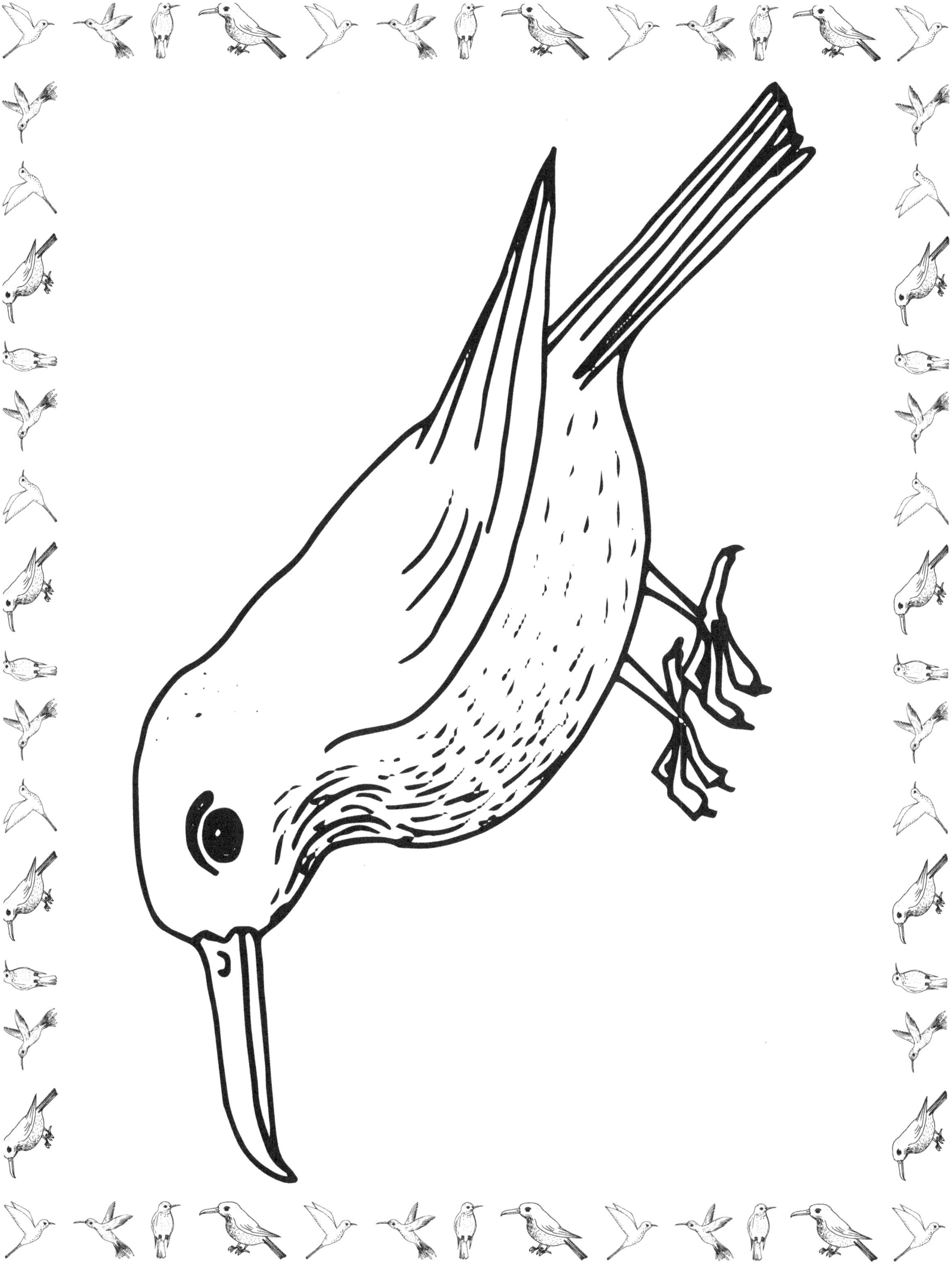

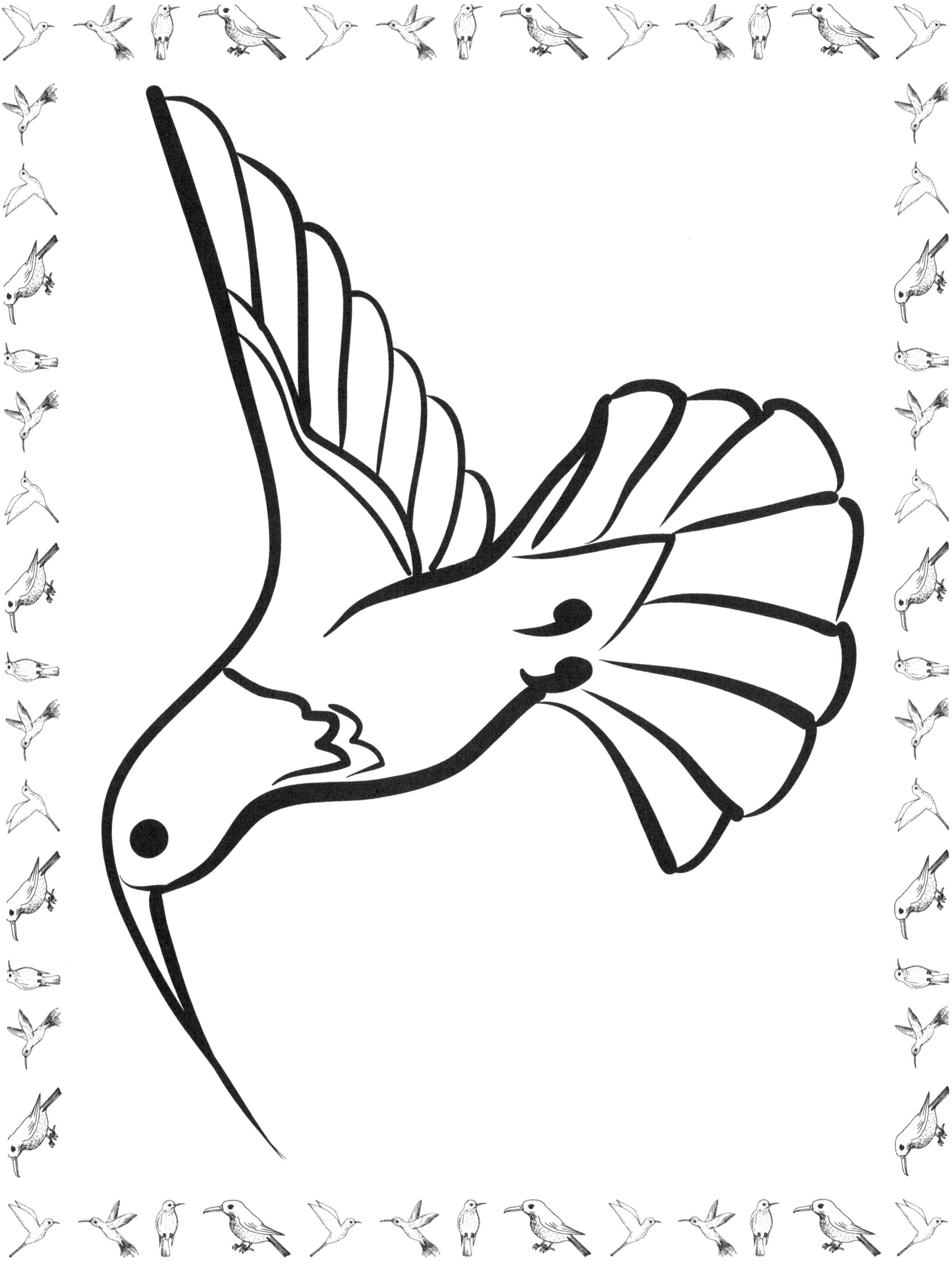

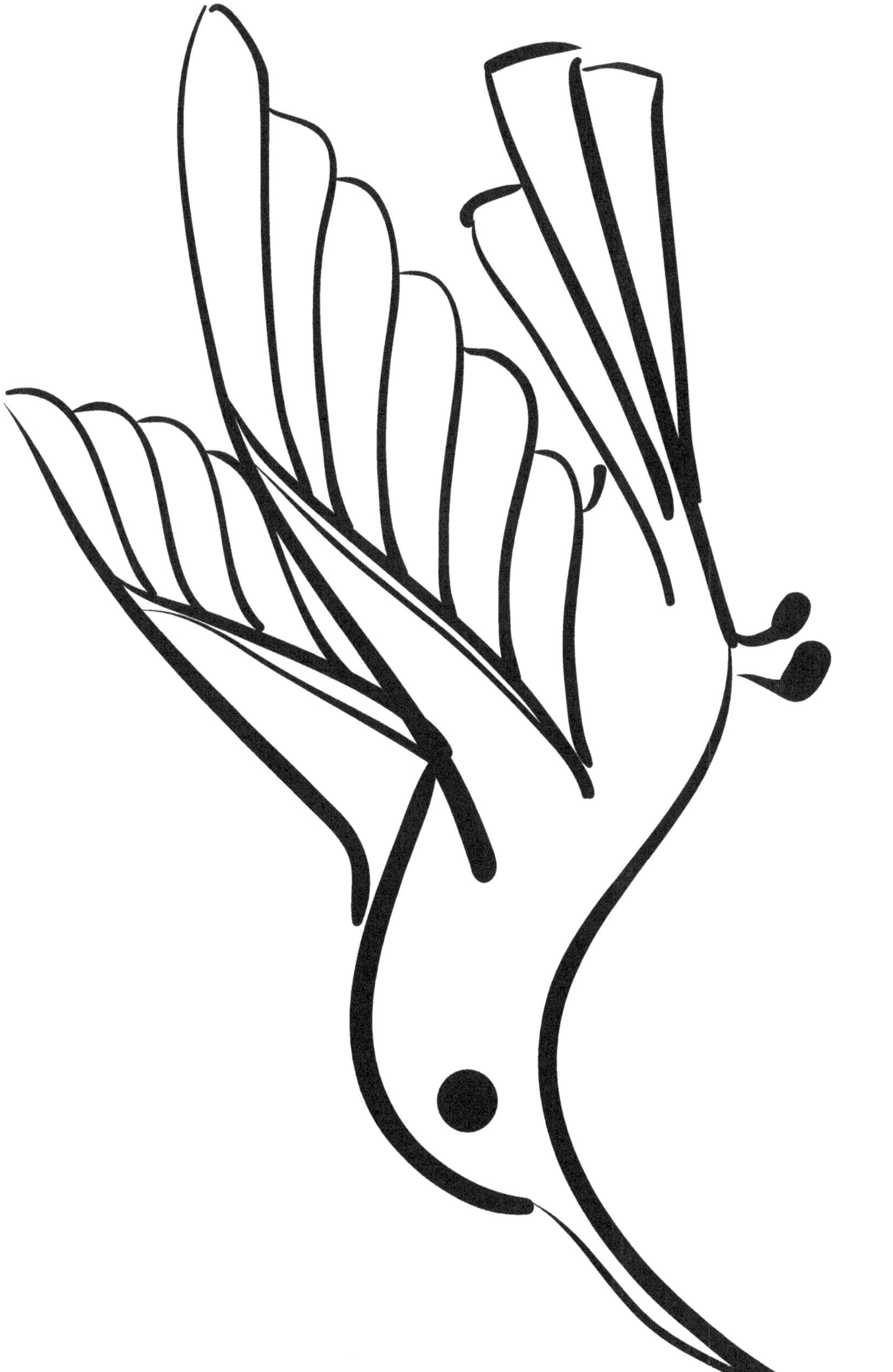

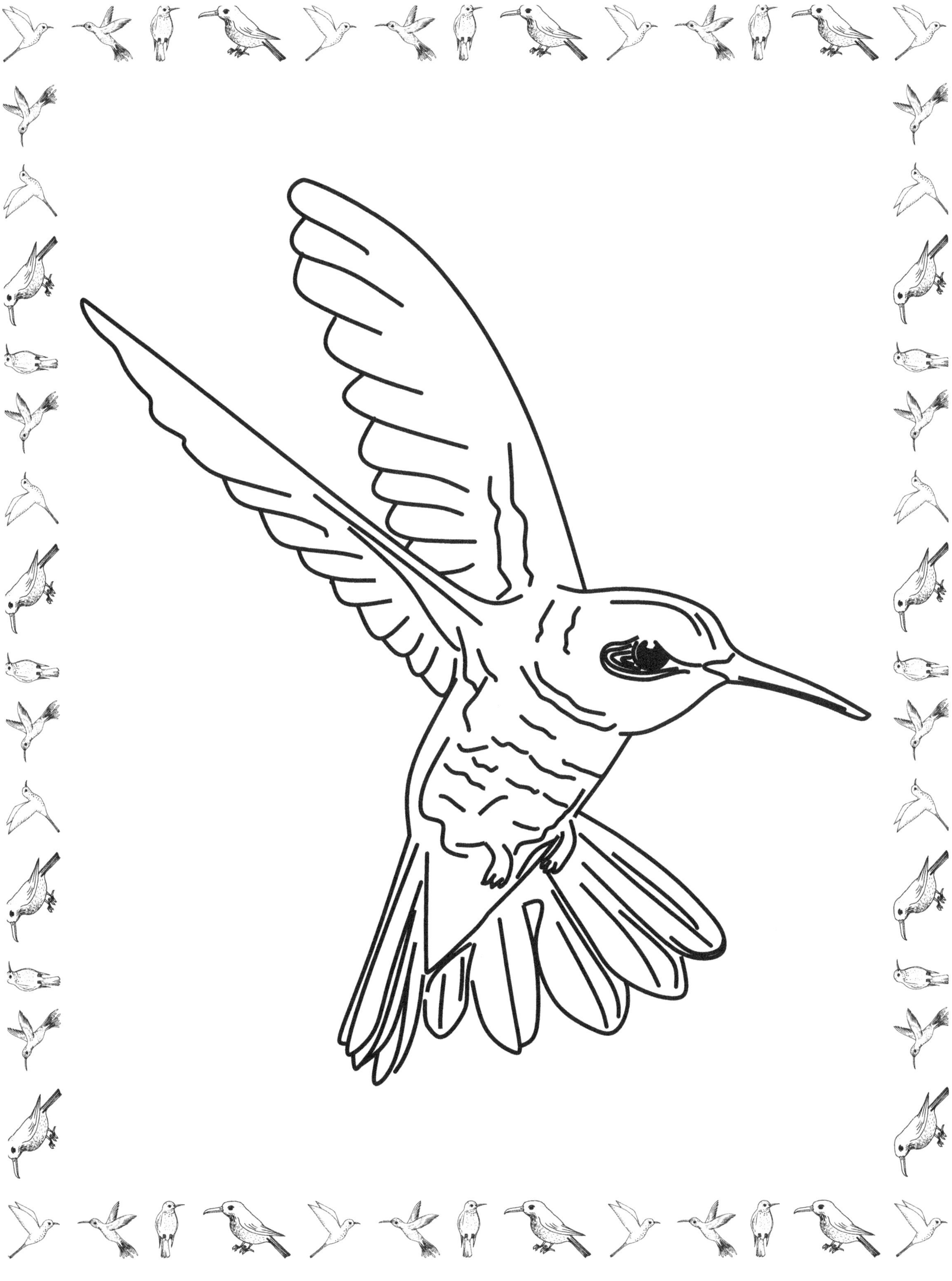

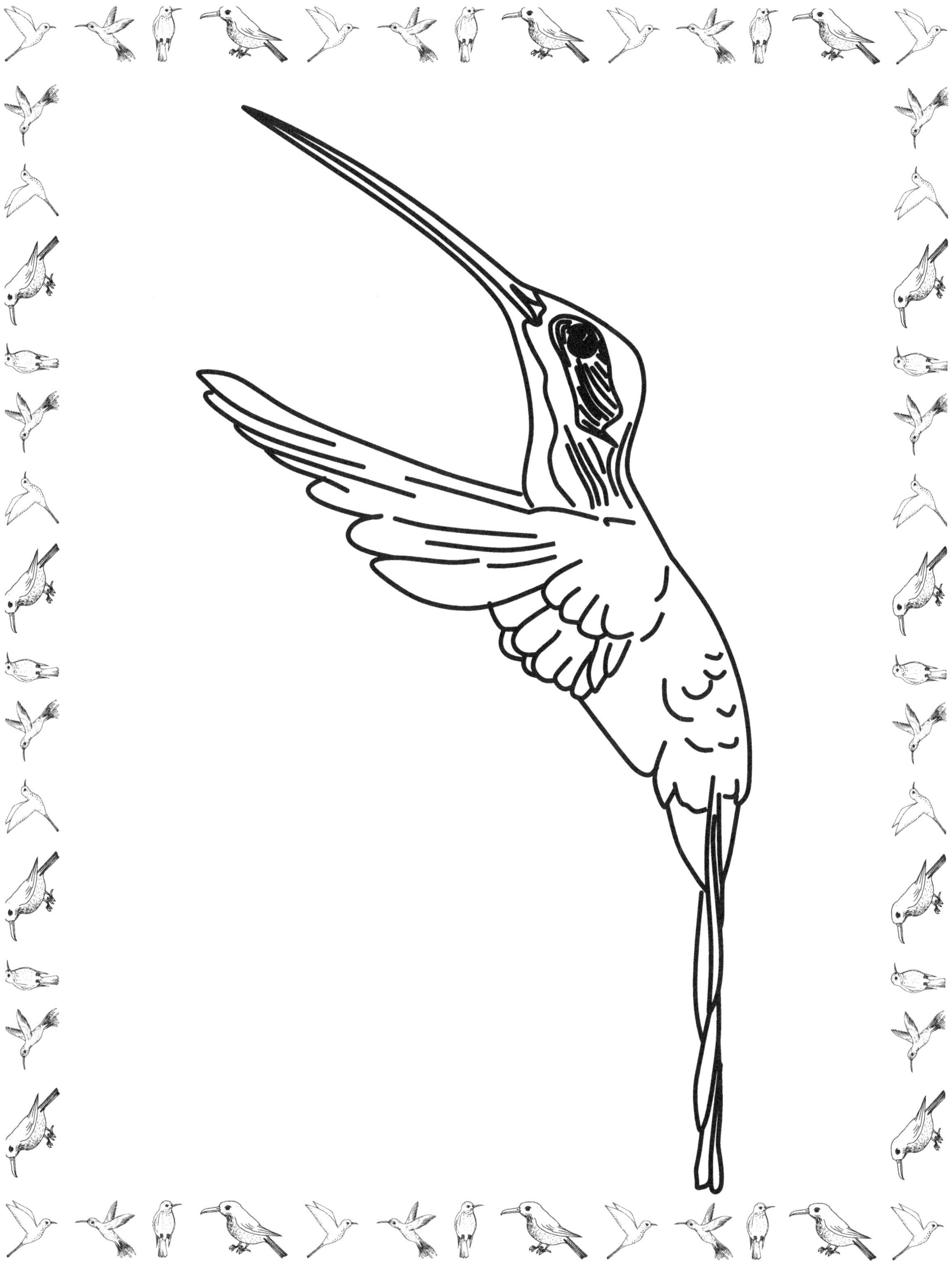

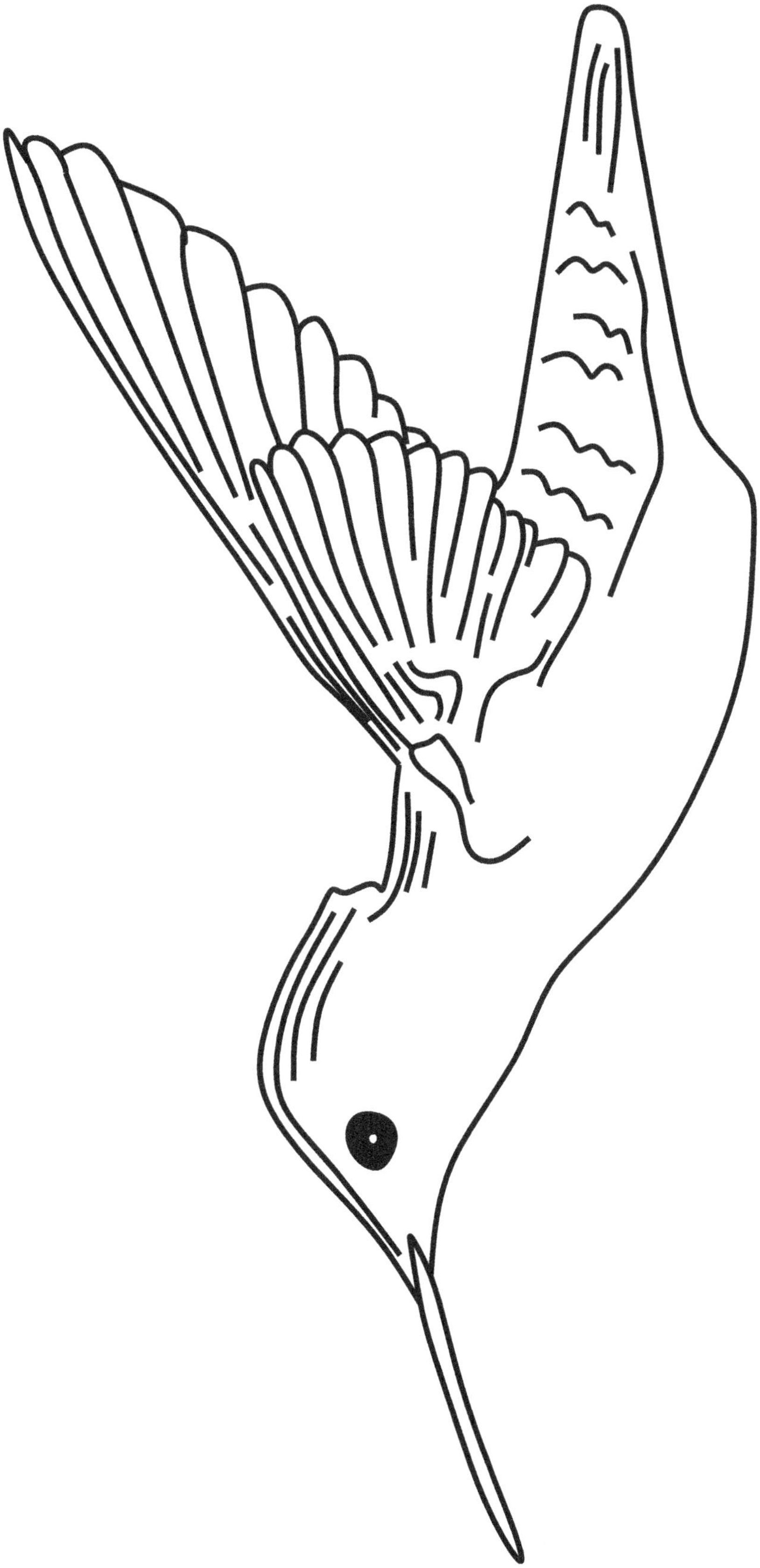

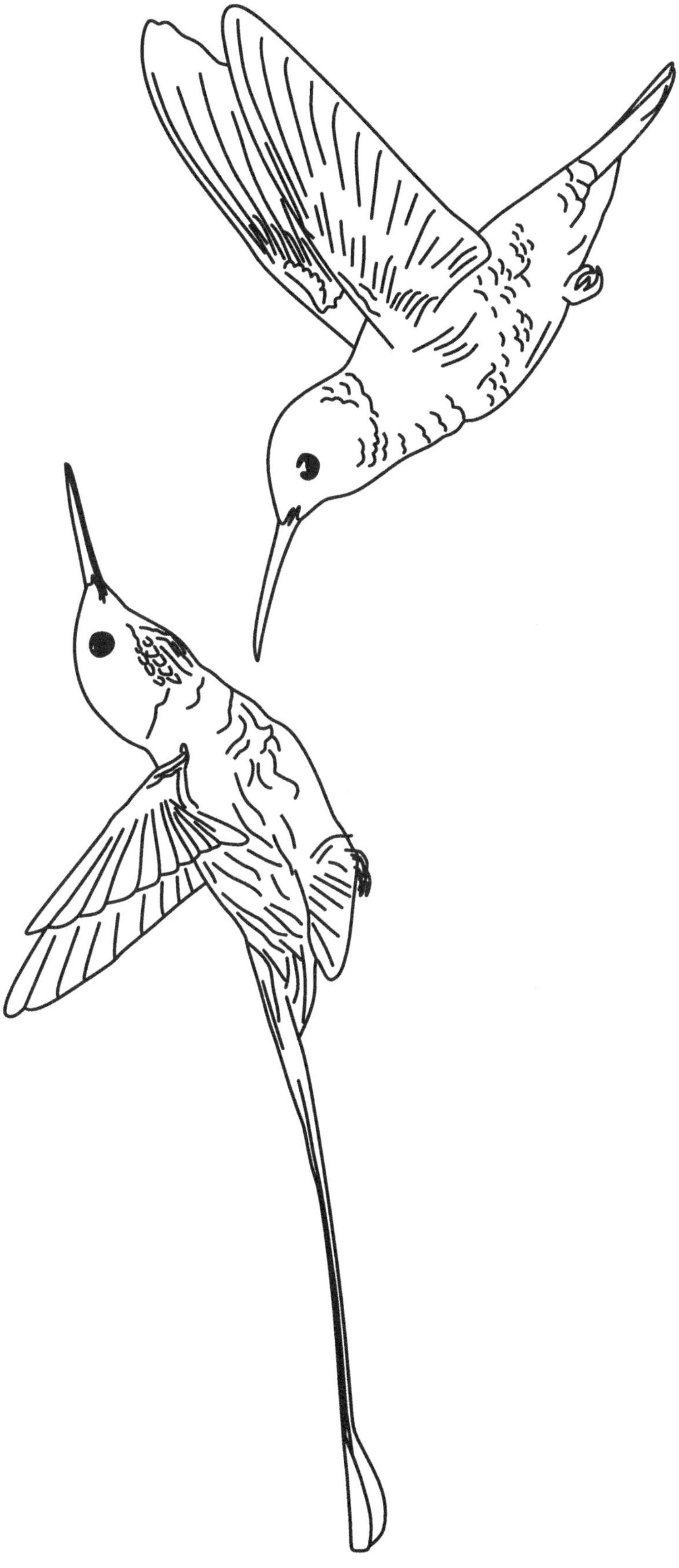

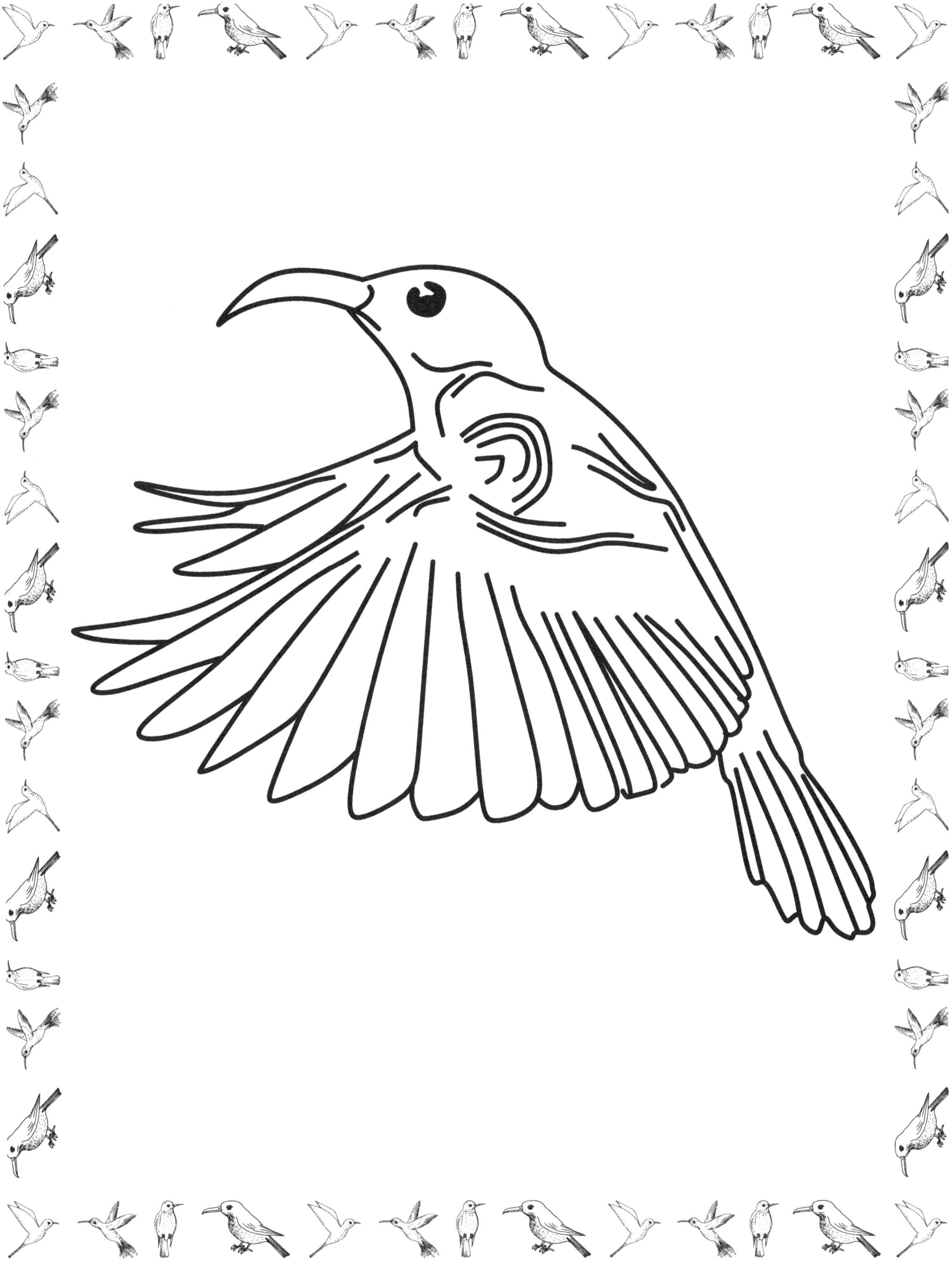

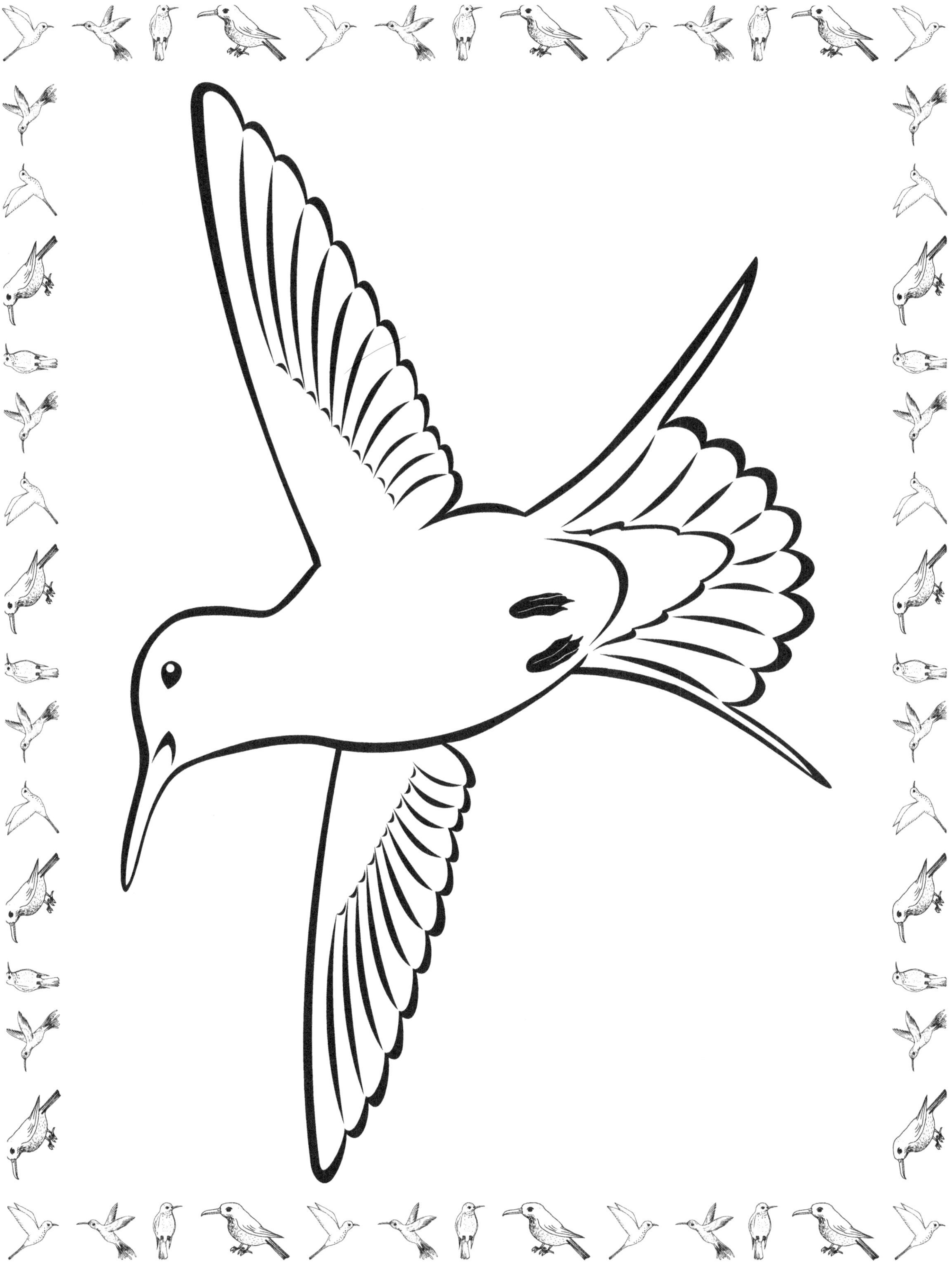

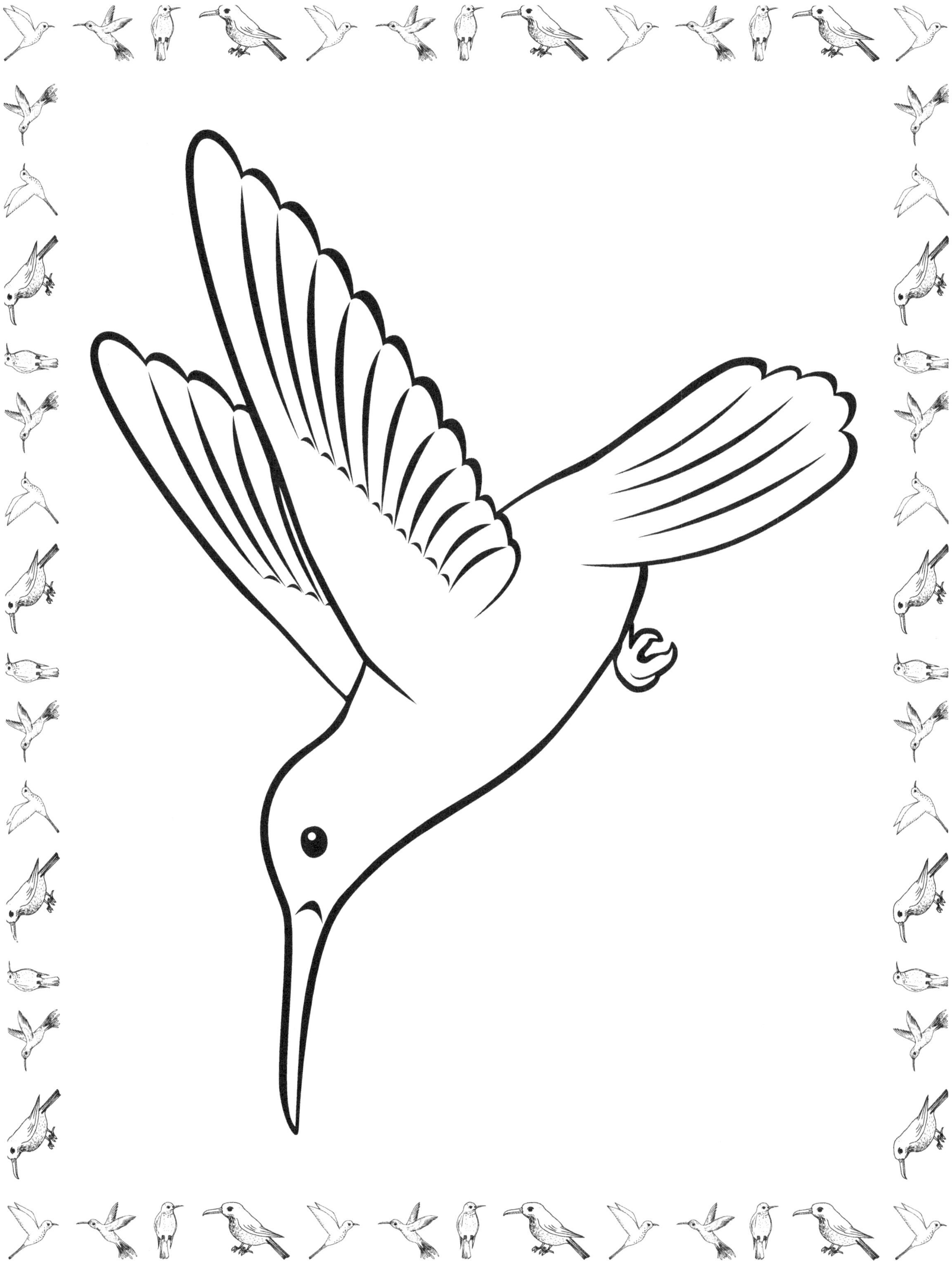

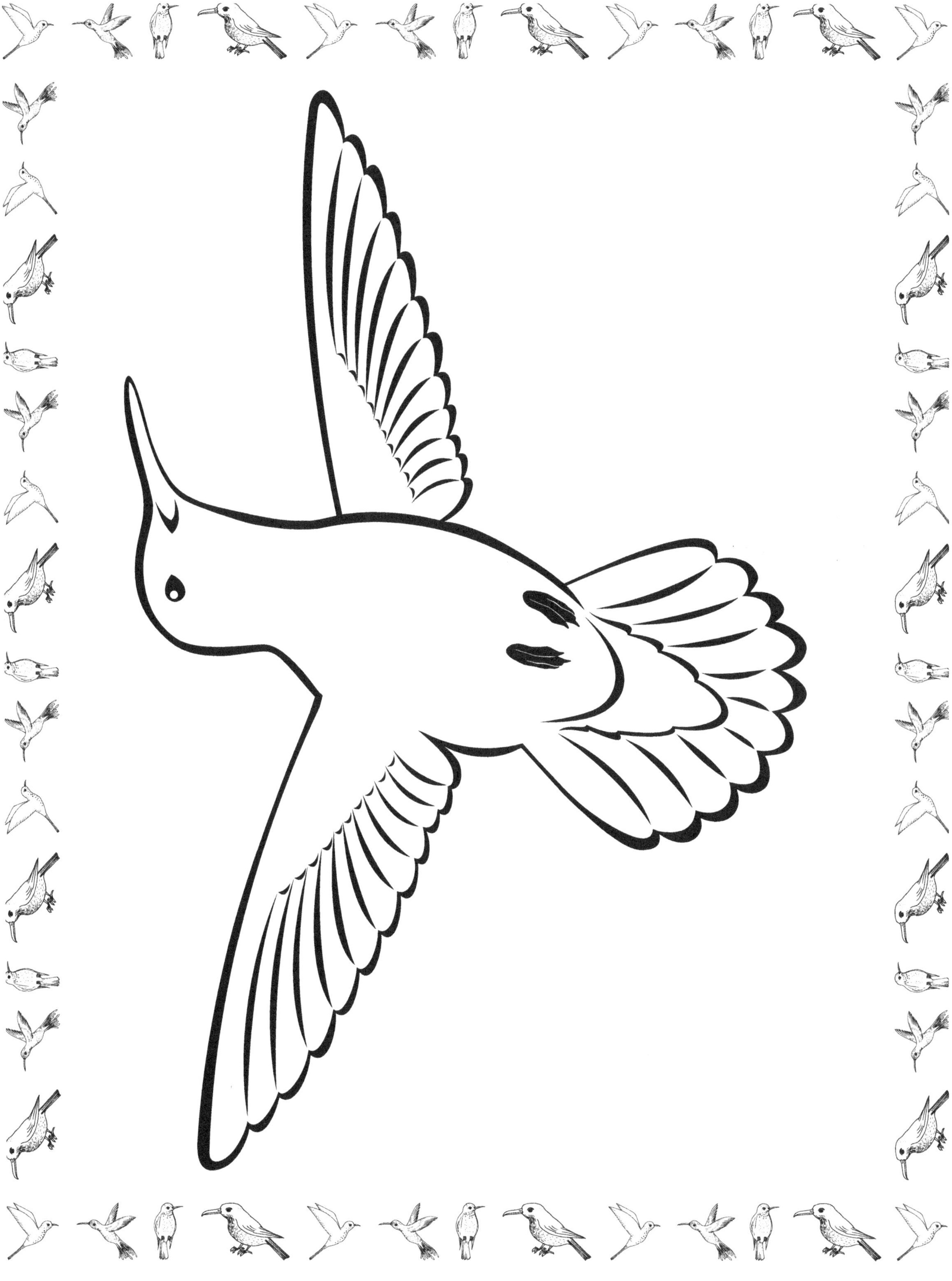

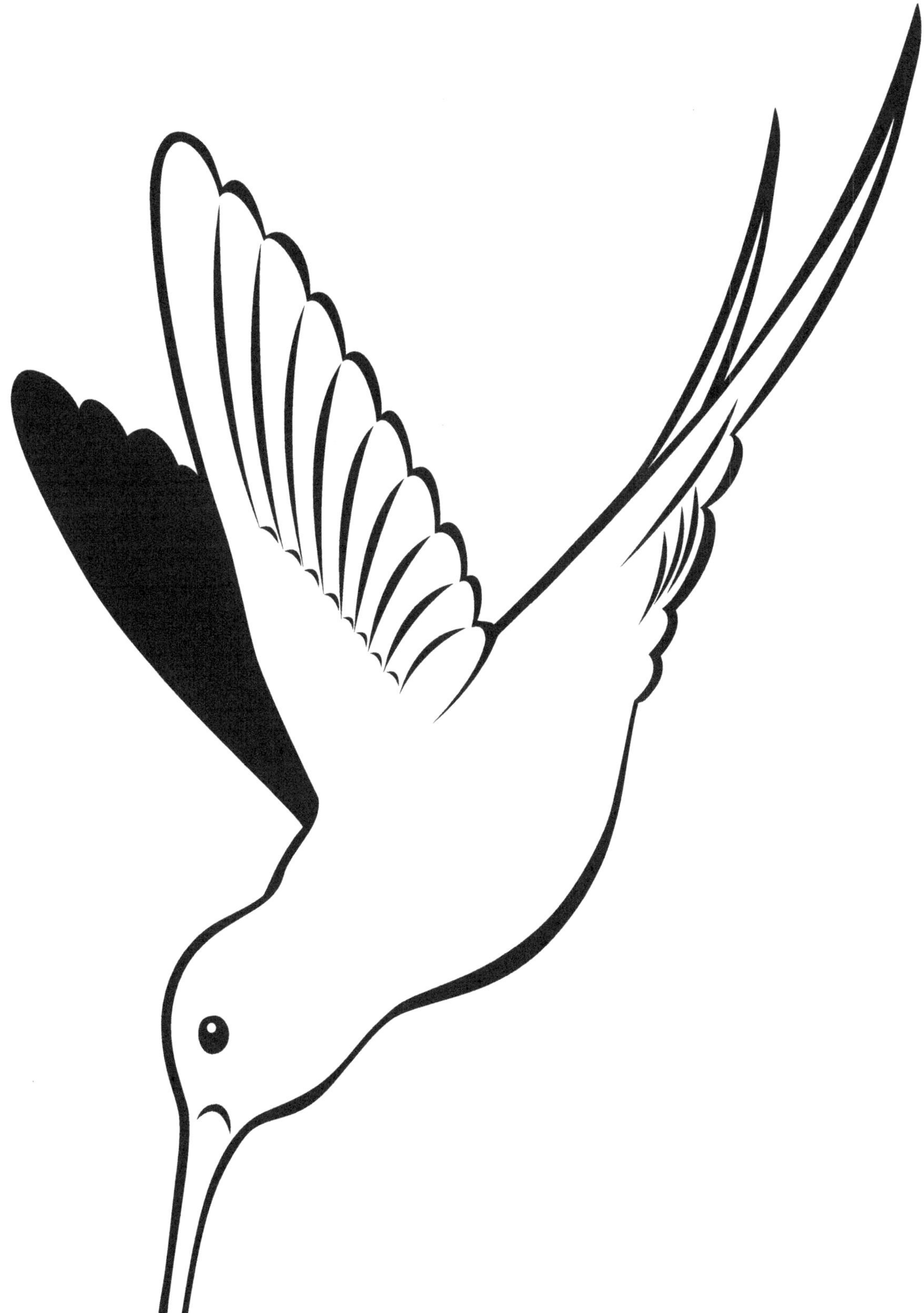

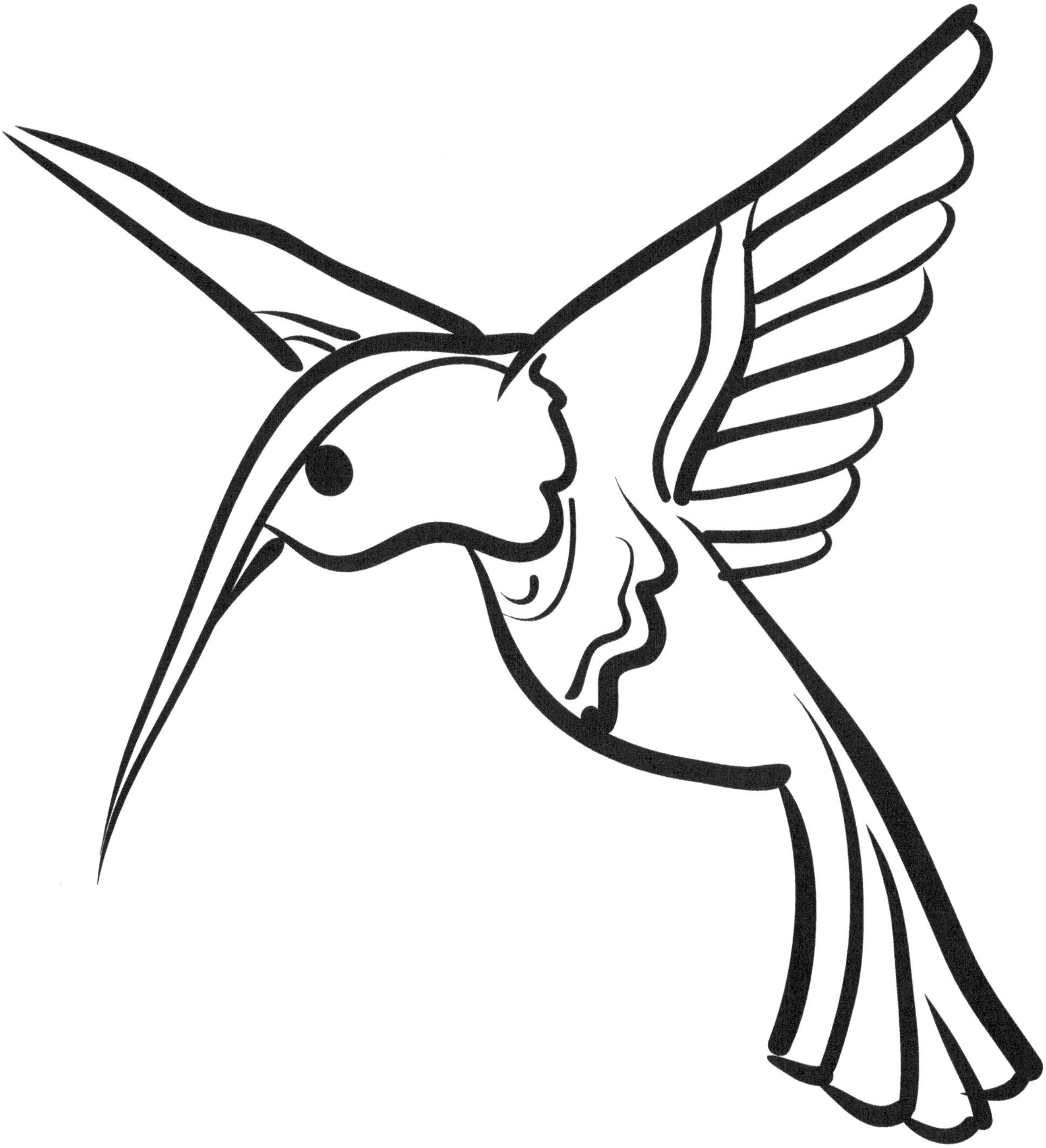

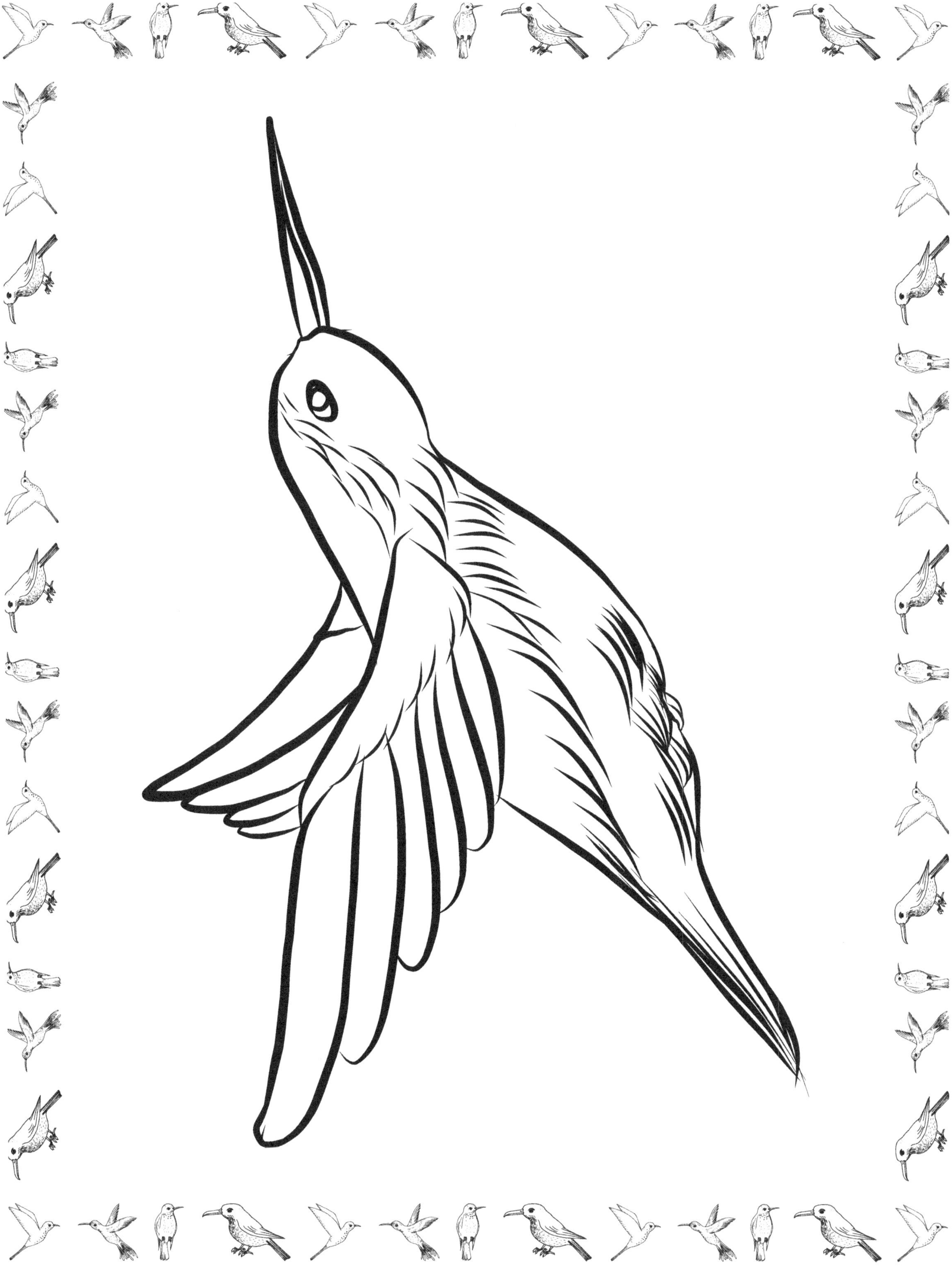

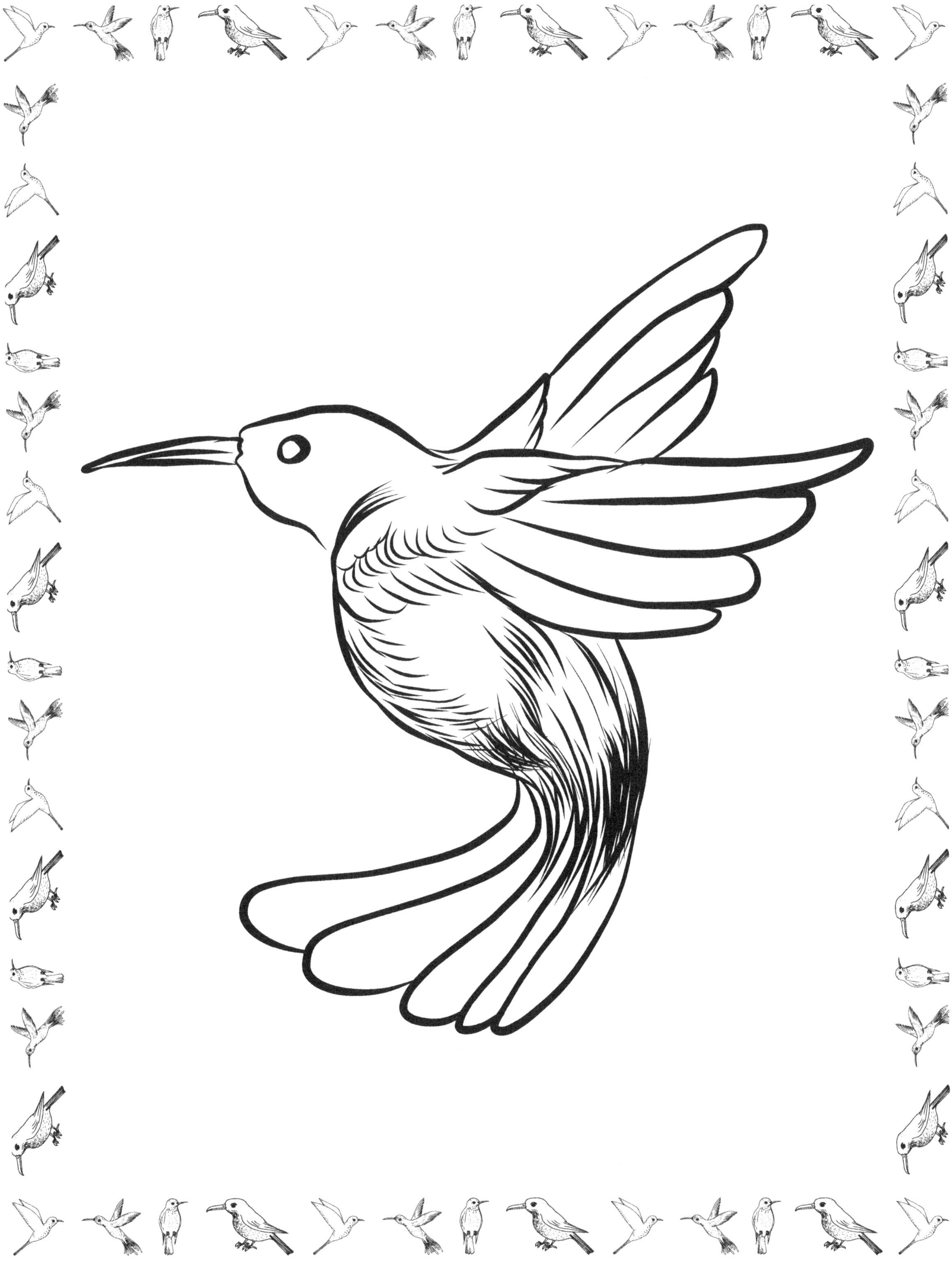

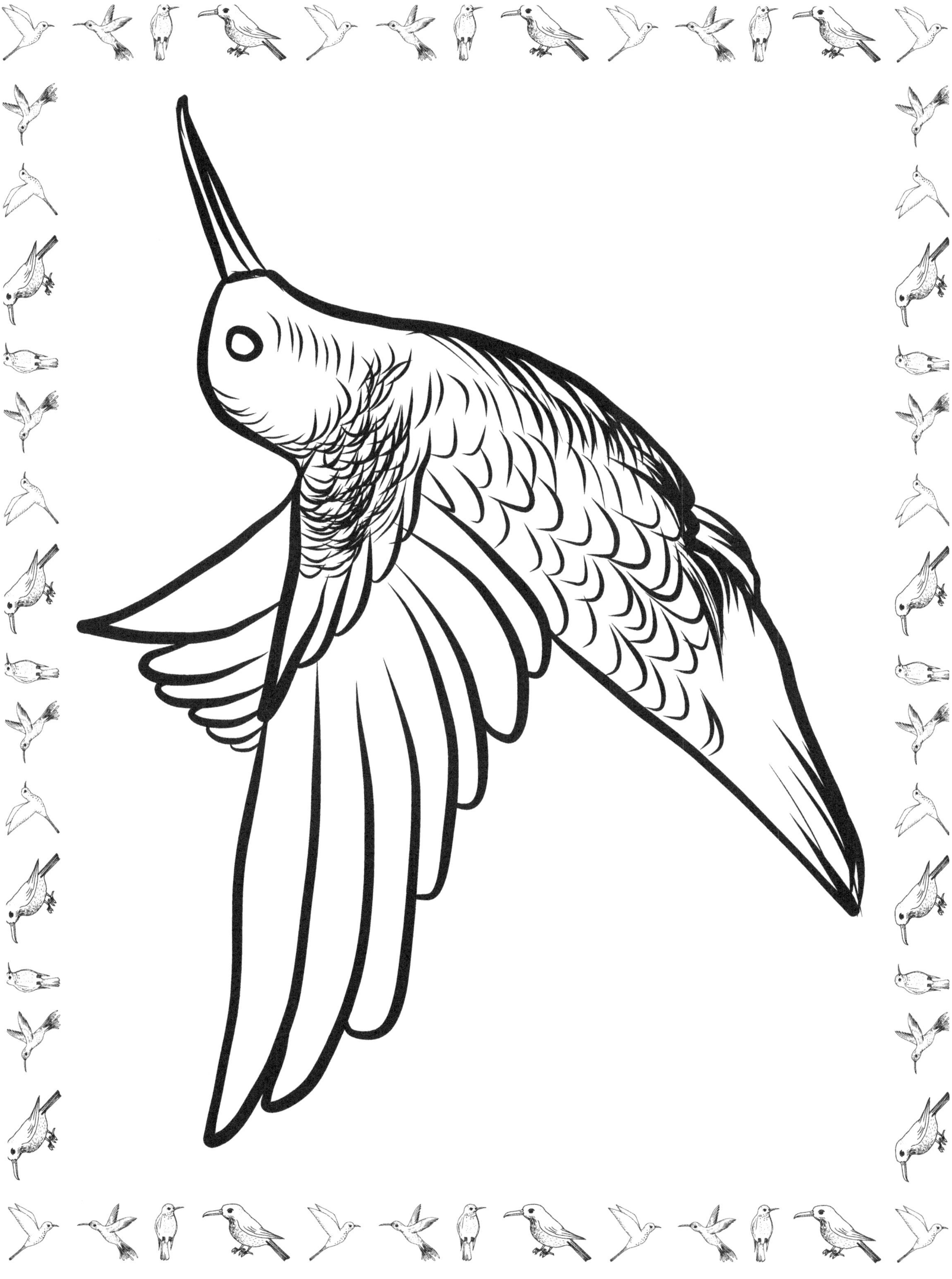

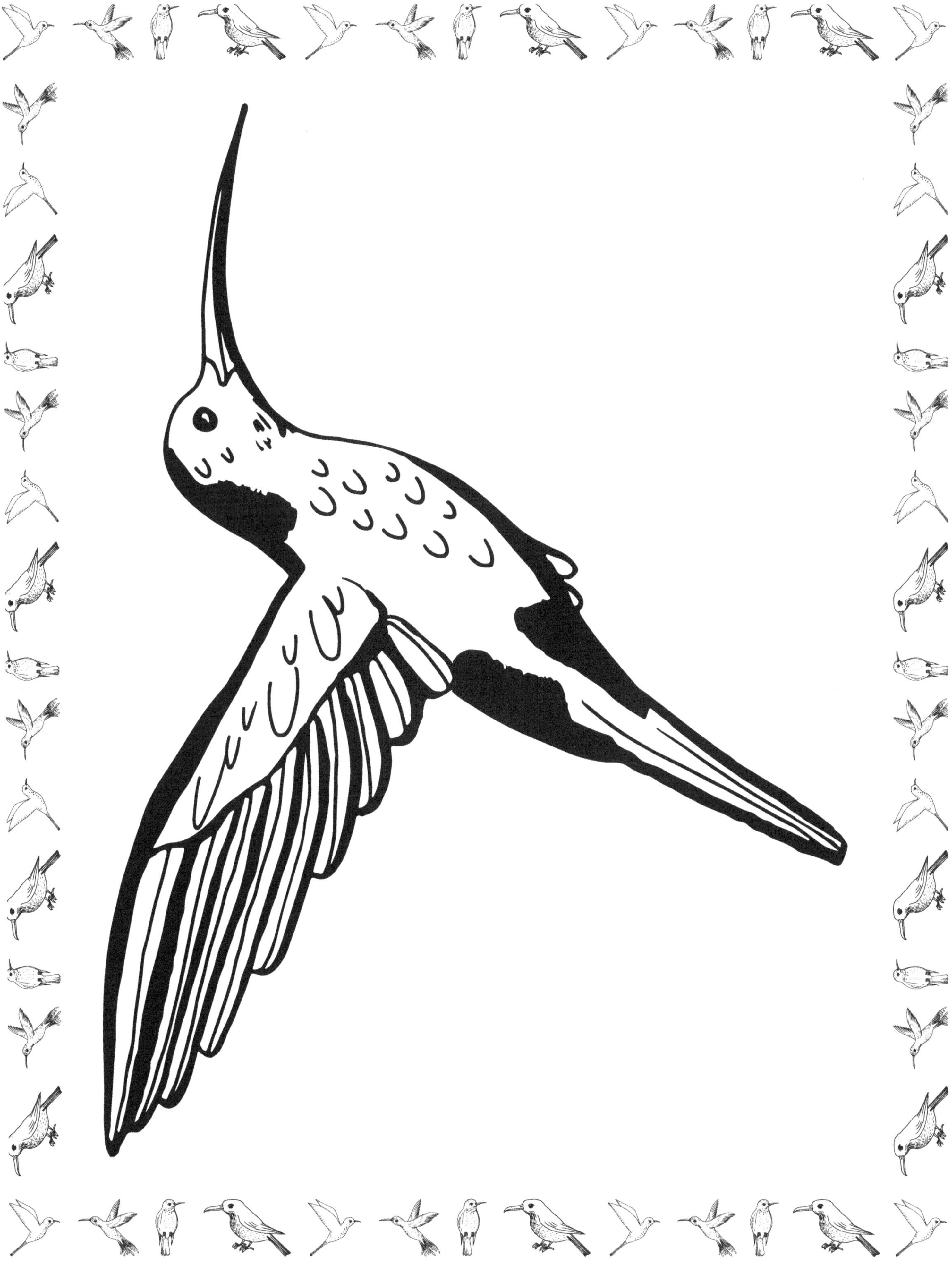

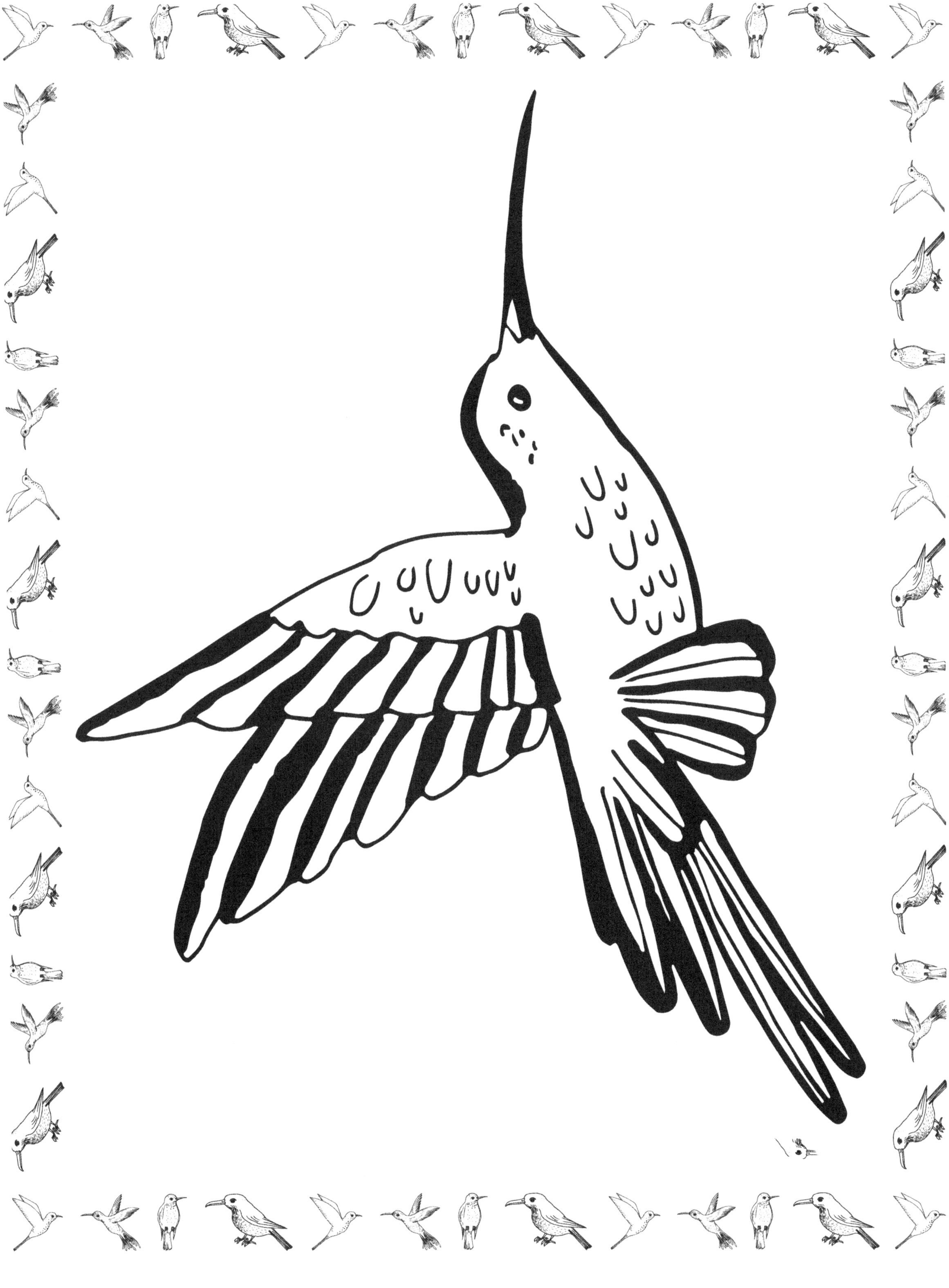

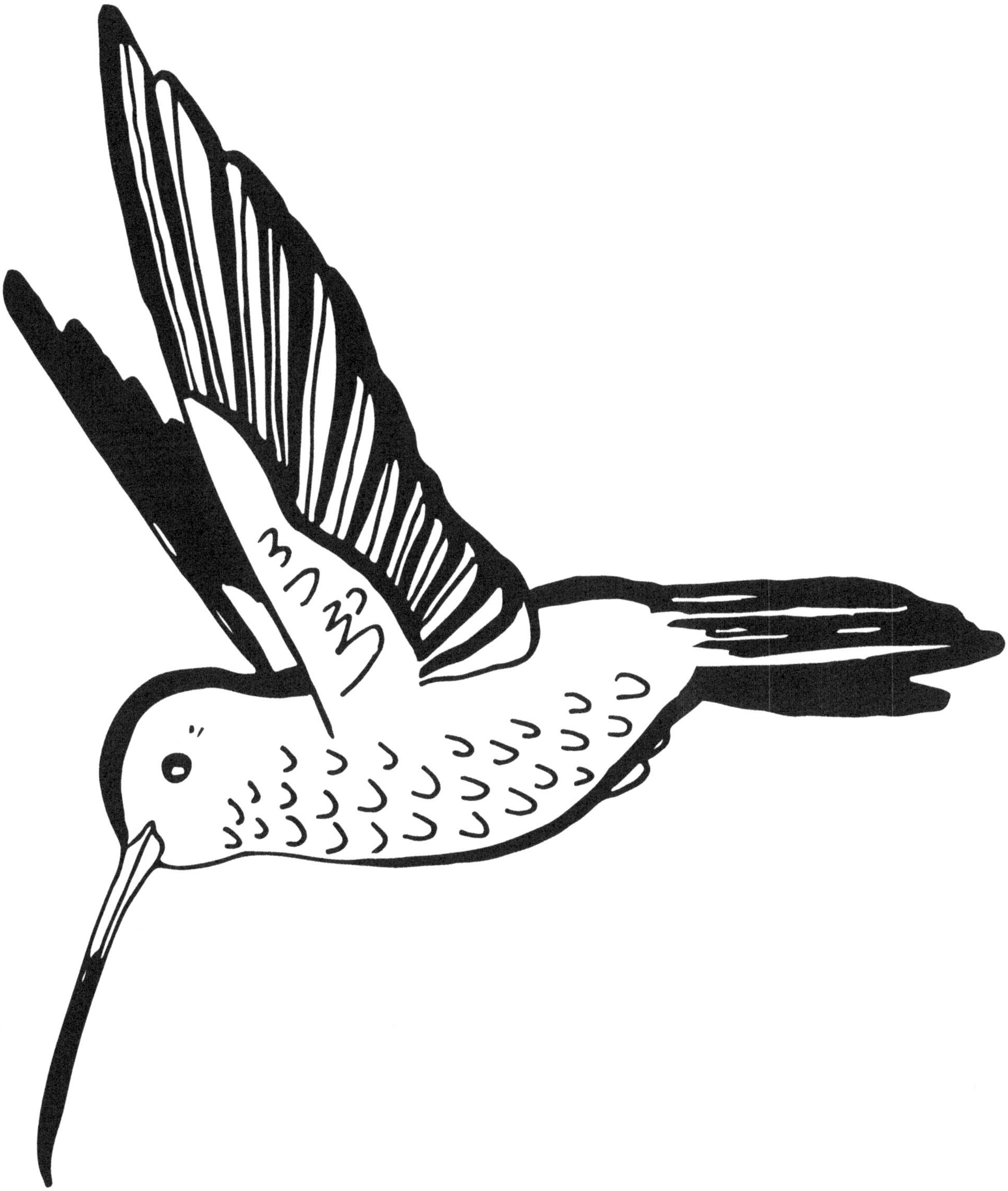

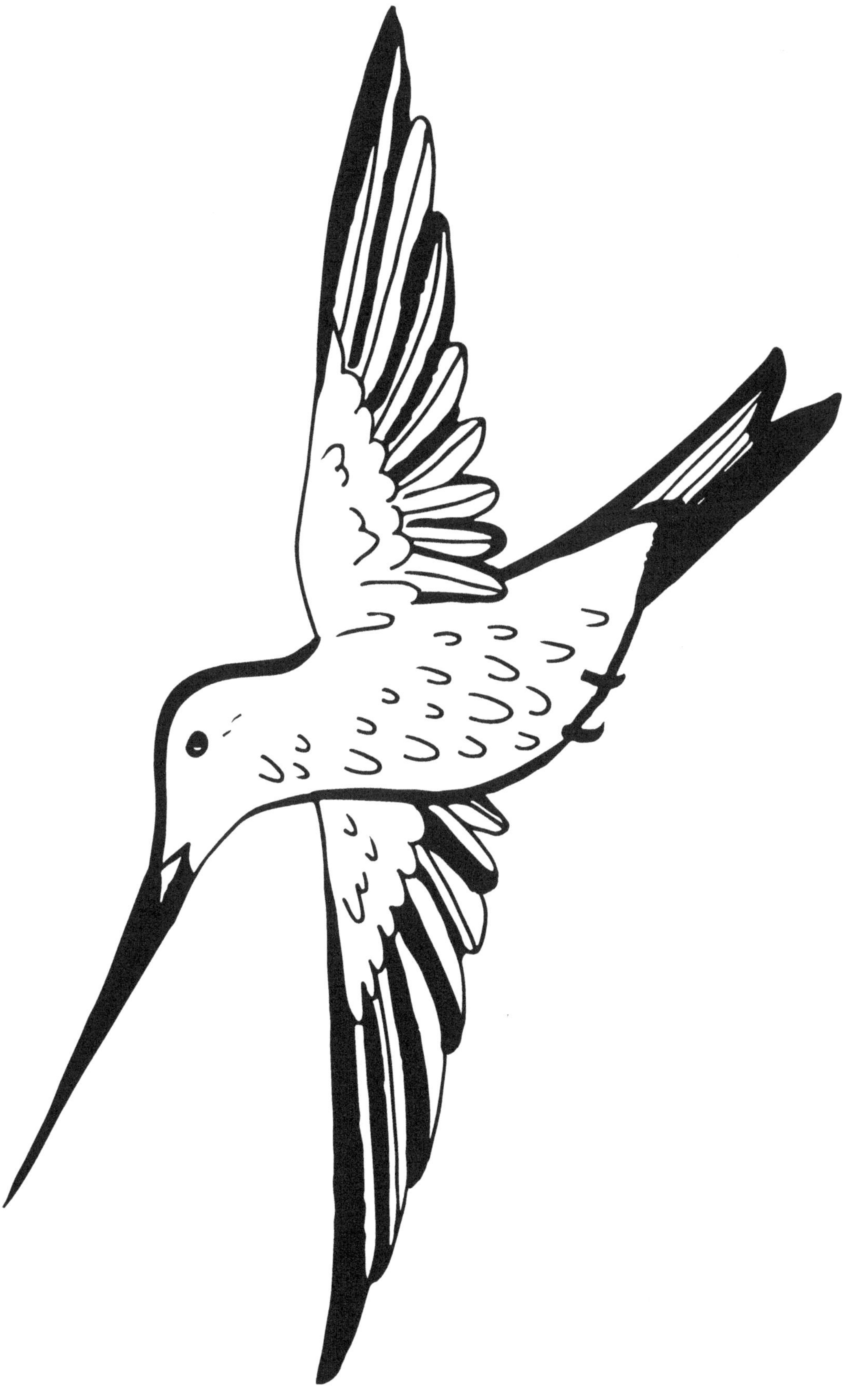

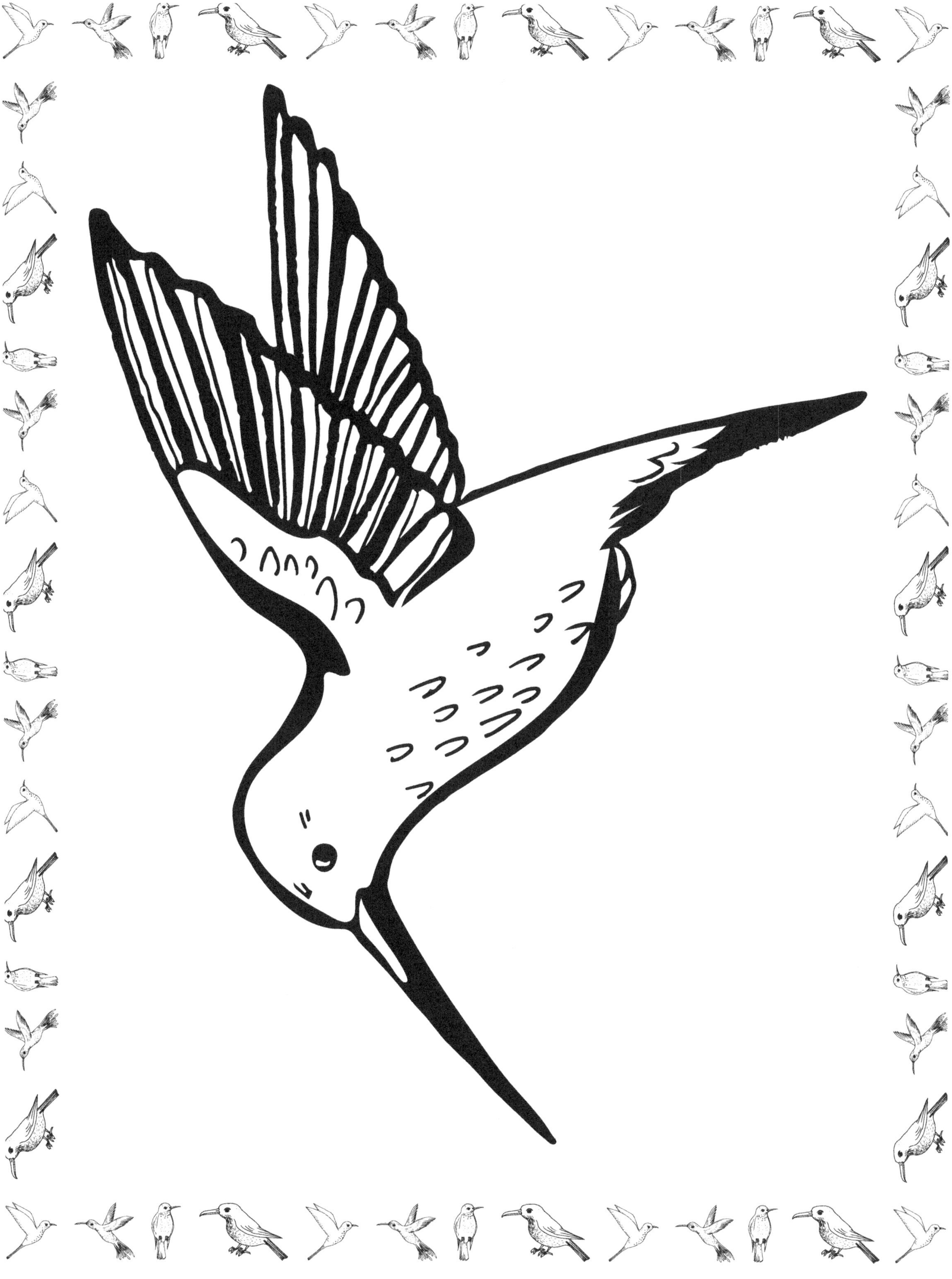

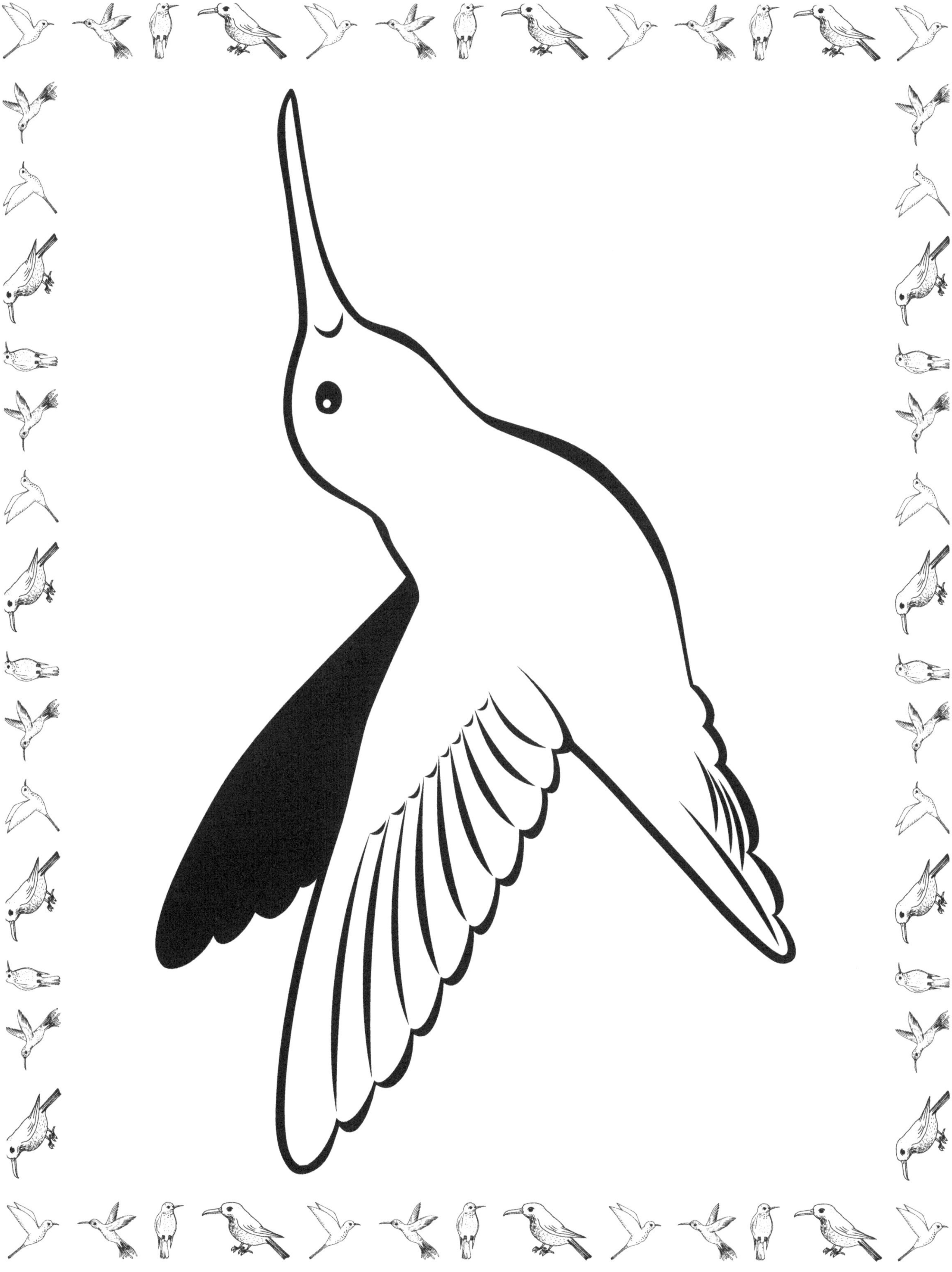

Made in the USA
Coppell, TX
25 May 2020

26418169R00039